THE SUPERMARKET REVOLUTION AND FOOD SECURITY IN NAMIBIA

NDEYAPO NICKANOR, LAWRENCE KAZEMBE, JONATHAN CRUSH AND JEREMY WAGNER

SERIES EDITOR: PROF. JONATHAN CRUSH

URBAN FOOD SECURITY SERIES NO. 26

ACKNOWLEDGEMENTS

The project on South African Supermarkets in Growing African Cities is funded by the Open Society Foundation for South Africa (OSF-SA). We wish to thank the following for their assistance with the project and this report: Gareth Haysom, Maria Salamone, Cameron McCordic, Bronwen Dachs and Ichumile Gqada. The IDRC and SSHRC are acknowledged for their support of the Hungry Cities Partnership and Consuming Urban Poverty 2 Project and for contributing in-kind resources to this project.

Published by the African Food Security Urban Network (AFSUN) and Hungry Cities Partnership (HCP)
www.afsun.org and www.hungrycities.net

First published 2017

ISBN 978-1-920597-28-3

Cover photo: Jonathan Crush

Production by Bronwen Dachs Muller, Cape Town

Printed by Print on Demand, Cape Town

AUTHORS

Ndeyapo Nickanor is Dean in the Faculty of Science at the University of Namibia, Windhoek.

Lawrence Kazembe is Associate Professor in the Department of Statistics and Population Studies, Faculty of Science, University of Namibia, Windhoek.

Jonathan Crush is CIGI Chair in Global Migration and Development, International Migration Research Centre, Balsillie School of International Affairs, Waterloo, Canada.

Jeremy Wagner is a Research Fellow at the Balsillie School of International Affairs, Waterloo, Canada.

Previous Publications in the AFSUN Series

CONTENTS

TABLES

FIGURES

"We recognize the urgent need to act now at local and national levels to address the challenges in food and nutrition security our country is facing today and ensure food and nutrition security for future generations" (Windhoek Declaration, July 2014)

1. INTRODUCTION

Rapid urbanization in Africa has been accompanied by a major transformation in national and local food systems. Thomas Reardon and colleagues were the first to argue that this transformation was being driven by a "supermarket revolution" that involved increasingly greater control over food supply and marketing by international and local supermarket chains (Reardon et al 2003, Weatherspoon and Reardon 2003). The current situation in Africa has been called the "fourth wave" of supermarketization in the Global South (with the others being in Latin America, Asia, and some African countries such as South Africa) (Dakora 2012). The transformation is driven by the development of new urban mass markets and the profit potential offered to large multinational and local supermarket chains (Reardon 2011). The restructuring of urban food systems by supermarkets involves "extensive consolidation, very rapid institutional and organizational change, and progressive modernization of the procurement system" (Reardon and Timmer 2012).

Integral to the process of food system restructuring is a simultaneous "quiet" or "grass-roots" revolution in urban food supply chains with tens of thousands of small and medium scale enterprises (SMEs) involved in trucking, wholesale, warehousing, cold storage, first and second stage processing, local fast food, and retail (Reardon 2015). These two views of food system revolution – one emphasizing the domination of supermarkets over supply chains from farm to fork and the other emphasizing the plethora of opportunities for small businesses in agri-food chains – are likely to vary in relative importance from place to place depending on local context.

The notion of the inevitability of a supermarket revolution in Africa was driven by at least three arguments – first, that there are "stages" of revolution and that the power of supermarkets in the Global North, and increasingly in Latin America, would inevitably diffuse to Africa (Reardon et al 2003, 2007). South Africa, whose entire food system has been revolutionized by a few supermarket chains, supposedly showed the rest of the continent a mirror of its own future. Second, the aggressive expansion of South African supermarkets into the rest of Africa after the end of apartheid was both symptomatic of and would hasten the realization of an African supermarket revolution (Miller et al 2008). Third, dietary change led by Africa's growing middle class was providing a massive new consumer market that only supermarkets were equipped to meet. Still, some researchers were sceptical, cautioning against the over-optimism and inevitability of the supermarket revolution model for Africa, the speed of the spread of supermarkets, and their potentially disruptive impact on traditional forms of retail (Abrahams 2009, 2011, Humphrey 2007, Vink 2013). Abrahams (2009) even suggested that "supermarket revolution myopia" neglected evidence of other potentially transformative processes and the resilience of informal food economies in Africa. The transition towards supermarkets is not a smooth evolution, nor does it entail the end of the informal food economy: "the growth and dominance of supermarkets presents only one element of a larger, more resilient narrative" (Abrahams 2009: 123).

The research and policy debate on the relationship between the supermarket revolution and food security focuses on four main issues:

- Whether supermarket supply chains and procurement practices mitigate rural food insecurity through providing new market opportunities for smallholder farmers;
- The potential negative impact of supermarkets on the urban informal food sector and its inefficient supply chains;
- The impact of supermarkets on the food security and consumption patterns of residents of African cities; and
- The relationship between supermarket expansion and governance of the food system, particularly at the local municipal level.

Each of these issues frames the context and questions of this report on South African supermarkets in Namibia. Against the backdrop of these themes, the project looks at the drivers and impacts of the expansion of South African supermarket companies into the rest of Africa. The larger project, of which this is a part, focuses on five African countries: Botswana, Mozambique, Namibia, Zambia and Malawi. This report presents the findings from research in 2016-2017 in Windhoek, Namibia, and addresses the following questions:

- What are the drivers of South African supermarket expansion within South Africa and what are the corporate strategies of the supermarket chains in relation to the rest of Africa?
- Which South African supermarkets are in Namibia? What locations do they occupy within Windhoek and how does this relate to high and low-income consumers? What are the implications for the acces-

sibility (geographical and economic) of urban consumers (including the urban poor) to these outlets?

- How are the supermarket supply chains organized? To what extent do they involve the import of products from South Africa and international markets? Are any products derived from Namibian sources and, if so, which?

- What are the patronage patterns of supermarkets by different income groups in Windhoek and what is the impact on food security of low-income groups (including food availability, accessibility, stability and nutritional quality of diets)?

- What is the impact of supermarket expansion on the informal food economy and what kinds of relationships exist between formal and informal markets and vendors and supermarkets?

The first section of this report reviews current information about the four key issues identified above relating to the supermarket revolution in Africa. The next section examines the structure and organization of the South African supermarket sector. It also examines the spatial strategies of supermarkets in urban areas and the debate on the impact of supermarkets on the informal food sector. This is important background since Namibia is increasingly integrated into and impacted by the organization and corporate strategies of the South African supermarket sector. The report then discusses the nature and drivers of South African corporate expansion into the rest of Africa and demonstrates that supermarket chains are leaders in this post-apartheid process. It identifies the major supermarket chains and their footprint in Africa and reviews some of the criticisms of the South African supermarket presence outside South Africa. The remaining sections of the report discuss the research findings in Namibia.

2. THE SUPERMARKET 'REVOLUTION'

As noted above, the debate on the supermarket revolution addresses four main areas. Regarding the relationship between smallholders and supermarkets, the international food security agenda has focused for more than a decade on improving the production and productivity of smallholder farmers, or what used to be called "rural development" (Crush and Frayne 2011a, Crush and Riley 2017). In the context of supermarket-driven change, the question is whether smallholders might be integrated into the vertically integrated operations that characterize the operations of supermarkets and, as a consequence, whether rural food security might be improved (Reardon 2009).

The initial prognosis was optimistic, as evidenced by the work of the Regoverning Markets Project (Vorley et al 2008, Biénabe et al 2011) and AGRA (the Alliance for a Green Revolution in Africa). However, various case studies have since sounded a discordant note (Dawson et al 2016; Gengenbach et al 2017). As Karaan and Kirsten (2008) note in the case of South Africa, "large food and agribusiness companies and large retailers are now dominant players in the South African agricultural and food system. This is replicating the situation in the high income industrialised nations of the world. Added to these realities are the low engagement levels of South African agribusiness and retailers with black farmers." The prospect of large-scale integration of smallholders into supermarket supply chains has become increasingly pessimistic, not just in South Africa (van der Heijden and Vink 2013), but also in other African countries (Andersson et al 2015, Muchopa 2013), Latin America (Blandon et al 2009, Michelson et al 2012) and Asia (Moustier et al 2010, Trebbin 2014). Increasingly, the consensus seems to be that the supermarket model is "inherently hostile towards smaller producers" (van der Heijden and Vink 2013: 68).

The second area of debate about the supermarket revolution concerns the relationship between the formal and informal food retail sectors. The conventional wisdom is that the spread of supermarkets will inevitably displace and even eradicate more traditional informalized supply chains and vendors, destroying livelihoods and increasing unemployment in the process. Kennedy et al (2004: 1), for example, argue that "competition for a market share of food purchase tends to intensify with entry into the system of…large multinational fast food and supermarket chains. The losers tend to be small local agents and traditional food markets." Reardon and Gulati (2008: 17) similarly assert that "the mirror image of the spread of supermarkets is the decline of the traditional retail sector." Louw et al (2007: 25) argue that in South Africa "one of the primary threats is the encroachment of supermarkets into areas traditionally occupied by the informal market." A contrasting position is that the informal food landscape in the South is extremely resilient in the face of competition. In Brazil, for example, Farina et al (2005) argue that "different formats of retail stores live together in the Brazilian market, compete for consumer preference and, at the same time, complement each other." Similar arguments about the complementarity of supermarkets and the informal food sector have been made in a number of Asian countries (Gorton et al 2011, Huang et al, 2015, Minten et al 2010, Schipmann and Qaim 2011, Si et al 2016, Suryadarma et al 2010, Zhang and Pan 2013).

A third general area of debate is the relationship between supermarket growth and urban food security. Standard FAO definitions suggest that food security has four main pillars: food availability, food accessibility, food utilization (including food safety) and food stability. Proponents argue that supermarket supply chains improve food security across all four dimensions by increasing the quantity and variety of foodstuffs available in urban areas, making food more accessible by reducing food prices through economies of scale, introducing quality controls that enhance food safety, and ensuring a stable food supply that is not subject to seasonal fluctuations or periodic shortages (Reardon et al 2003). There is general agreement that supermarket supply chains have the potential to improve food availability and food stability. However, there is little consensus about their impact on the accessibility and utilization dimensions of food security. Much of the global research on supermarket impacts on food security has focused on food utilization, diet and nutrition. There is incontrovertible evidence that the Global South is undergoing a dietary transition leading to a double (undernutrition and overnutrition) burden of malnutrition (Popkin et al 2012). Across the Global South, including Africa, the prevalence of overweight, obesity and accompanying noncommunicable diseases (NCDs) is increasing rapidly (Popkin and Slining 2013).

The key question is whether and how supermarkets are implicated in this process. Several studies suggest that supermarkets are driving dietary change, unhealthy food choices and the consumption of ultra-processed foods, and contributing to the obesity pandemic and NCDs (Asfaw 2008, Hawkes 2008, Igumbor et al 2012, Kelly et al 2014, Monteiro et al 2011, Umberger et al 2015). Others suggest that the impact of supermarkets is variable. Gómez and Ricketts (2013) argue that negative dietary change is confined to higher-income groups and that there is "little nutritional impact" among the urban poor. Peyton et al (2015) argue that in Cape Town, however, supermarkets do impact negatively on the urban poor, primarily because they carry a narrow range of fresh food products and focus on the marketing of cheap, processed foods that are energy-dense, fatty, sugary and salty. Kimenju et al (2015) conclude that although supermarkets and their food sales strategies in small-town Kenya contribute to changing food consumption habits and nutritional outcomes, these impacts differ by age cohort and initial nutritional status. As a result, "simple conclusions on whether supermarkets are good or bad for nutrition and public health are not justified."

The final area of debate about supermarkets relates to the policy implications of supermarket expansion in urban food markets. Timmer (2009: 1816) suggests that the development policy issues presented by the supermarket revolution "cut across the entire economy, from agricultural technology and farmer responsiveness, to concentration in processing and retailing channels, to standards for food quality and safety, to food security at both micro and macro levels." The foundational policy issue confronting national governments throughout the Global South is whether to allow unfettered access to their consumer markets by supermarket chains. This issue was crystallized in Indian opposition to the penetration of multinational supermarkets and their potential negative impact on locally owned small-scale retailers and their supply chain intermediaries (Reardon and Minten 2011). In South Africa, a coalition of labour unions, consumer groups and local supermarket chains unsuccessfully opposed the takeover of Massmart by American retail giant Walmart, whose motive was to penetrate the profitable South African consumer market and use South Africa as a bridgehead into the rest of Africa (Dralle 2017, Kenny 2014, Parker and Luiz 2015). The related question for national African governments is what policies to adopt towards direct foreign investment by South African supermarkets; a question that cannot be separated from their policies towards direct investment by South African companies in general, which spans the whole continent and numerous economic sectors (Berkowitz et al 2012).

Timmer (2009) argues that "there are few policy implications that are specific to managing the supermarket revolution" but that it does affect the food policy agenda in two basic ways: (a) at the micro or household level through the impact of supermarkets on poor consumers; and (b) at the macro-level through the impact of supermarkets on staple food supplies, price stability and links to external markets. National policy makers should also be concerned about how to influence the behaviour of supermarkets "in ways that serve the interests of important groups in society, especially small farmers and the owners of traditional, small-scale food wholesale and retail facilities" (Timmer 2009: 1814). Reardon and Hopkins (2006) suggest that it is the role of government to proactively manage the "emerging tensions" among supermarkets, suppliers and traditional suppliers. Ruel et al (2017) are optimistic about the desire and capacity of policy to enable positive food security outcomes. Timmer (2017) recently suggested that "government policies can shape both the positive and negative dimensions (of supermarket expansion) at the margin, but most of the dynamics of supermarket growth are stimulated by technological changes and consumer demands that are beyond the control of governments." In many African countries, unconditional national and municipal support for modern supermarket retail expansion accompanies efforts to curtail or erase the informal food sector (Skinner 2016). This raises the question of what kinds of policies are in place to manage the urban food system and food retail environment at the city level. Researchers in Africa have argued that coherent city-level urban food security policies are largely absent and, where they do exist, they focus primarily on promoting urban agriculture (Brown 2015, Haysom 2015, Smit 2016).

3. SOUTH AFRICA'S SUPERMARKET REVOLUTION

3.1 Urban Food and Corporate Control

Retail is the third largest sector on the Johannesburg Stock Exchange (JSA) ranked by turnover, with six firms featuring in the top 40 (Figure 1) (das Nair and Dube 2017). Five of the six retailers in the top 40 are supermarket chains – Shoprite Holdings (14th), Massmart Holdings (Walmart) (16th), the Spar Group (20th), Pick n Pay Stores (23rd) and Woolworths Holdings (27th), while the sixth is furniture retailer Steinhoff (Table 1). Financial turnover for the listed supermarkets increased significantly between 2010 and 2015.

FIGURE 1: Number of Firms by Sector in JSE Top 40, 2015

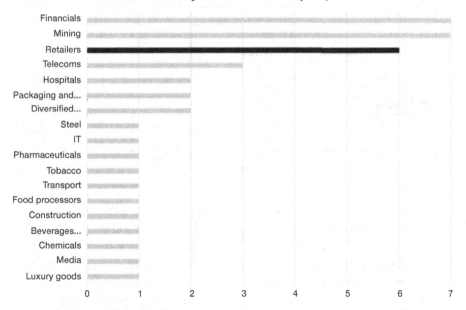

Source: das Nair and Dube (2017)

	Company	Sector	2010 Turnover	2015 Turnover	Increase/ Decrease
	TABLE 1: JSE Top 30 by Turnover (ZAR billion), 2010 and 2015				
1	Glencore	Mining	1,813	2,653	840
2	BHP Billiton	Mining	404	636	232
3	Anglo American	Mining	184	318	134
4	British American	Tobacco	153	299	146
5	SABMiller	Beverages/brewers	131	269	138
6	Sanlam	Financials	123	239	116
7	Bidvest Group	Industrials	110	205	95
8	Sasol	Chemicals	122	185	63
9	MTN Group	Telecoms	115	147	32
10	Old Mutual	Financials	70	145	75
11	Steinhoff International	Retailers	48	137	89
12	Richemont SA	Luxury goods	48	136	88
13	Mondi Limited	Packaging/paper	55	115	60
14	Shoprite Holdings	Retailers	67	114	47
15	Imperial Holdings	Transport	54	110	56
16	Massmart Holdings	Retailers	47	85	38
17	Vodacom Group	Telecoms	59	77	18
18	Datatec	IT	29	75	46
19	Sappi	Packaging/paper	46	75	29
20	Spar Group	Retailers	35	73	38
21	Naspers	Media	28	73	45
22	Anglogold Ashanti	Mining	262	67	-195
23	Pick n Pay Stores	Retailers	55	67	12
24	Standard Bank Group	Financials	38	65	27
25	Barloworld	Industrials	42	63	21
26	Anglo Platinum	Mining	46	60	14
27	Woolworths Holdings	Retailers	26	57	31
28	Liberty Holdings	Financials	22	54	32
29	Aveng	Construction	34	44	10
30	FirstRand	Financials	18	40	22
Source: das Nair and Dube (2017)					

Greenberg (2017) identifies three developments that facilitated the concentration of corporate power in the South African food retail system: (a)
the Uruguay Round of GATT (leading to the formation of the WTO
and locking countries into trade agreements with implications for production and distribution systems); (b) the dismantling of the South African
statutory regulatory systems governing agricultural products and their
replacement with a combination of greater market forces and industry self-
regulation, embodied in the Marketing of Agricultural Products Act of
1996; and (c) amendments to the Cooperatives Act in 1993 that allowed
the cooperative infrastructure to be removed from farmer control and then

corporatized and privatized. These processes of privatization, trade liberalization, state deregulation and corporate self-regulation replaced the earlier apartheid-era system of state control and regulation. Together with rising consumer demand from urbanization, they fuelled the large-scale expansion of a new corporate agro-food system within the country (Bernstein 2013). Corporate retailing and the supermarket became the pre-eminent format to market food to consumers (Greenberg 2017).

The transformation of South Africa's food system by supermarket corporations has involved extensive consolidation, rapid institutional and organizational change throughout entire agro-food value chains, and progressive technological modernization of their procurement systems. The structures of South African supermarkets and their value chains have changed and expanded over time, shifting from serving affluent consumers in urban areas to new markets in lower-income communities (Peyton et al 2015). Power in the food retail environment has been consolidated primarily by local companies. South African-based corporate entities such as Pick n Pay and Shoprite were able to expand rapidly in high-income areas, becoming dominant players in the food retail industry. These companies adopted many of the strategies of their North American and European counterparts, utilizing supply chain formalization and Western-style layouts to establish a ubiquitous supermarket format (Peyton et al 2015). The country's retail outlets now offer a variety of formats similar to those in the United States and, in the process, the agro-food system and its value chains have been restructured. Figure 2 provides a diagrammatic overview of the South African agro-food system and highlights the significant corporate actors in the food value chain.

The largest food sector activity is wholesale and retailing, followed by manufacturing and then primary production (Greenberg 2017). Food passes through specific stages of activity and value is added as it moves downstream. Downstream stages along the value chain are larger in terms of value than those upstream (Figure 3). The five big food retailers in South Africa, which are also the five largest retailers across all sectors (Shoprite, Pick n Pay, Spar, Massmart and Woolworths), had a combined profit of ZAR14.5 billion in 2014 (Greenberg 2017). Combined, they control two-thirds of the total South Africa food retail market and their profit is nearly three times that of the top five food processors. Although processors may seek to shape demand through the creation of new products, the buying power of supermarkets is the most significant force within the agro-industrial complex.

Large-scale supermarket chains dominate the food retail market in most South African urban areas as anchor tenants in malls and mini-malls, as stand–alone supermarkets on main streets, and along major transportation arteries. They also operate convenience-store formats including in petrol stations as well as chains such as OK MiniMark and Friendly stores. Whereas most food retailing in African countries is fragmented and consumers buy primarily from neighbourhood kiosks or independently owned convenience stores, South African consumers are an exception. South Africa's marketplace is much denser in terms of corporate retail, with the number of hypermarkets and supermarkets increasing from 790 in 2009 to 2,875 in 2015 (Nortons Inc 2016). In 2013, there was one store for every 16,000 people nationwide (Vink 2013). Branded convenience stores have also increased to more than 4,500 outlets. Despite accounting for only 5% of all retail outlets in number, supermarkets command over two-thirds of the market in South Africa (Nortons Inc., 2016).

FIGURE 2: The South African Agro-Food System

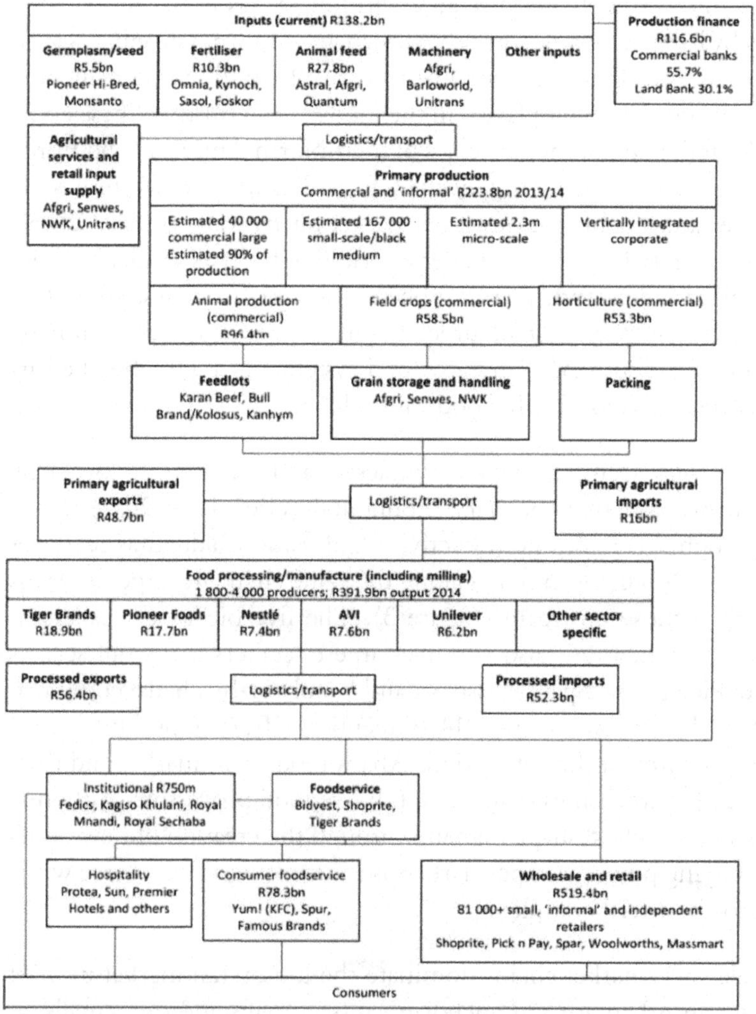

Inputs (current) R138.2bn					Production finance R116.6bn Commercial banks 55.7% Land Bank 30.1%
Germplasm/seed R5.5bn Pioneer Hi-Bred, Monsanto	Fertiliser R10.3bn Omnia, Kynoch, Sasol, Foskor	Animal feed R27.8bn Astral, Afgri, Quantum	Machinery Afgri, Barloworld, Unitrans	Other inputs	

Agricultural services and retail input supply Afgri, Senwes, NWK, Unitrans

Logistics/transport

Primary production Commercial and 'informal' R223.8bn 2013/14

Estimated 40 000 commercial large Estimated 90% of production	Estimated 167 000 small-scale/black medium	Estimated 2.3m micro-scale	Vertically integrated corporate

Animal production (commercial) R96.4bn	Field crops (commercial) R58.5bn	Horticulture (commercial) R53.3bn

Feedlots Karan Beef, Bull Brand/Kolosus, Kanhym	Grain storage and handling Afgri, Senwes, NWK	Packing

Primary agricultural exports R48.7bn — Logistics/transport — **Primary agricultural imports R16bn**

Food processing/manufacture (including milling) 1 800-4 000 producers; R391.9bn output 2014

Tiger Brands R18.9bn	Pioneer Foods R17.7bn	Nestlé R7.4bn	AVI R7.6bn	Unilever R6.2bn	Other sector specific

Processed exports R56.4bn — Logistics/transport — **Processed imports R52.3bn**

Institutional R750m Fedics, Kagiso Khulani, Royal Mnandi, Royal Sechaba	Foodservice Bidvest, Shoprite, Tiger Brands

Hospitality Protea, Sun, Premier Hotels and others	Consumer foodservice R78.3bn Yum! (KFC), Spur, Famous Brands	Wholesale and retail R519.4bn 81 000+ small, 'informal' and independent retailers Shoprite, Pick n Pay, Spar, Woolworths, Massmart

Consumers

Source: Greenberg (2017)

FIGURE 3: Value in the South African Agro-Food System, 2014

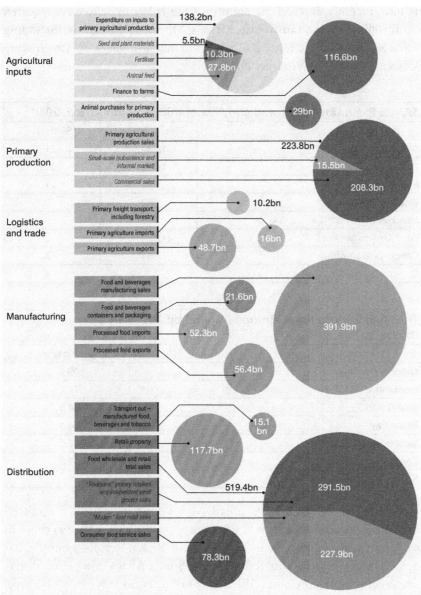

Source: Greenberg (2017)

In terms of store numbers, South Africa's food retail market is dominated by four large supermarket chains: Shoprite Holdings (31% share), Pick n Pay (30%), Spar (21%) and Woolworths (9%) (Table 2). The other significant South African chain is Fruit & Veg City's Food Lover's Market (around 2%). The top five supermarket retailers on the JSE can also be ranked in terms of their market capitalization (Table 3) (das Nair and Dube 2017). On this basis, Shoprite and Woolworths are the largest supermarket chains in the retail industry in South Africa. While food retail is dominated by locally owned corporations, two external players have recently entered the country. One is Walmart, which acquired a controlling interest in South Africa's Massmart Holdings (including Game Stores), and the other is Choppies, a much smaller but fast-growing Botswana-based supermarket chain.

TABLE 2: Number of Stores and Ownership in South Africa, 2016	No. of stores	Share %
Shoprite (SA)	1,284	31
Pick n Pay (SA)	1,280	30
Spar (SA)	890	21
Woolworths (SA)	382	9
Massmart/Walmart/Game (USA)	203	5
Food Lover's Market (SA)	(+100)	2
Choppies (Botswana)	64	2
Source: das Nair and Dube (2017)		

TABLE 3: Supermarket Groups Ranked by JSE Market Capitalization, 2016	ZAR billion
Shoprite Holdings	109.9
Woolworths Holdings	74.2
Spar Group	34.5
Pick n Pay	34.4
Massmart Holdings	32.6
Choppies Limited	4.3
Source: das Nair and Dube (2017)	

South African supermarket chains have invested heavily in centralized distribution centres that service in-country operations, as well as those in neighbouring countries, including Namibia. Pick n Pay, for example, has 11 distribution centres distributed across South Africa. Shoprite's distribution centre in Centurion is the largest on the continent (at 180,000m²), with over 1,100 suppliers and is the distribution point for 90% of ambient products delivered to stores in Gauteng province and beyond. Shoprite's five distribution centres in the Western Cape province are currently being consolidated into a single 120,000m² facility. Supermarket corporations either own their own vehicle fleets or outsource distribution of products to stores. Shoprite, for example, has its own transport fleet under the Freshmark name, while Pick n Pay outsources to Imperial Logistics. Supermarkets also obtain some of their products from wholesalers and hybrid retailers. Independent buying groups play a role in the food supply chain, selling both to independent retailers and wholesalers. The major buying groups include Unitrade Management Services, the Buying Exchange Company, the Independent Buying Consortium, the Independent Cash & Carry Group and Elite Star Training. Figure 4 illustrates the relationship between suppliers, buying groups, distribution centres and supermarkets (das Nair 2017).

FIGURE 4: Food Retail Supply Chains in South Africa

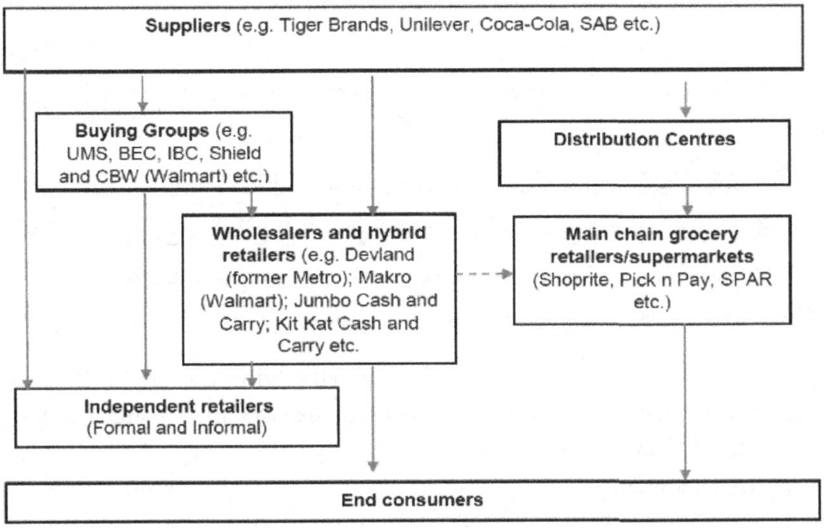

Suppliers (e.g. Tiger Brands, Unilever, Coca-Cola, SAB etc.)

Buying Groups (e.g. UMS, BEC, IBC, Shield and CBW (Walmart) etc.)

Distribution Centres

Wholesalers and hybrid retailers (e.g. Devland (former Metro); Makro (Walmart); Jumbo Cash and Carry; Kit Kat Cash and Carry etc.

Main chain grocery retailers/supermarkets (Shoprite, Pick n Pay, SPAR etc.)

Independent retailers (Formal and Informal)

End consumers

Source: das Nair (2017)

3.2 Consumer Markets and Supermarket Location

South Africa's supermarket sector is a low profit margin industry characterized by intense competition. With the exception of Woolworths, which targets a higher-income demographic (Figure 5), there are high levels of price competition across numerous categories of groceries. The major retailers compete in offering not only the lowest prices but also the most extensive range of products at the best value. The extent of the competition is so intense that some retail grocers have introduced programmes that match any price offered by competitors across a select group of stocked products. In-store design and formatting innovations are constantly being adapted to find a competitive advantage. Key food retail strategies include product diversification beyond just groceries, multi-channel approaches to reaching consumers, in-store financial services, larger format stores, format diversification (such as forecourts and convenience stores), and collection of consumer data to shape supply and demand (Greenberg 2017). The supermarket chains have all introduced their own brand/label products, e.g. Shoprite's Ritebrand and Housebrand in its Checkers stores, which cover approximately 300 products, and Pick n Pay's No Name brand (das Nair 2017: 17).

FIGURE 5: Price Competition Between Supermarket Chains, 2008-2016

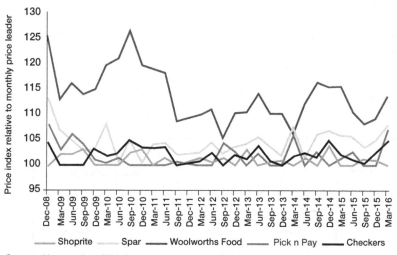

Source: Nortons Inc. (2016)

Supermarkets were once associated primarily with the small elite of upper-income residents of African cities, but are now increasingly targeting middle and low-income residents. In South Africa, budget subsidiaries of supermarket chains are penetrating low-income areas, often as anchor tenants in mini-mall developments (Peyton and Battersby 2014). In an AFSUN study of 11 cities in nine Southern African countries, over 80% of poor urban households procured some of their food from supermarkets (a figure higher than that for the informal sector) (Crush et al 2012). What is less certain is whether, and in what ways, greater geographical proximity impacts on other forms of accessibility, such as the cost of food relative to income. Supermarket competitors differentiate their products and marketing strategies on the basis of an assessment of their consumer base. Figure 6 uses a Living Standards Measure (LSM) to assess differentiation between the consumer bases of the major supermarket groups. Lower LSM categories indicate lower living standards whereas higher categories indicate higher living standards. Shoprite, Spar, and Pick n Pay cater primarily to the LSM 5-7 categories, with Pick n Pay targeting a higher proportion of LSM 8-10 consumers than the other two. Shoprite and Spar both serve more LSM 1-4 consumers than Pick n Pay, while Woolworths targets more LSM 8-10 consumers than Pick n Pay.

A spatial analysis of supermarket location in Cape Town found that supermarkets are most commonly located in middle-class neighbourhoods within the city (Peyton et al 2015). The study classified incomes into quintiles, with income group 1 being the lowest and 5 the highest. Income group 4 had the highest density of supermarkets per square kilometre (Figure 7). The lower three income groups, and particularly Group 1, have the lowest concentration of supermarkets and thus the lowest level of food provisioning from formal retail outlets. The supermarket density of Group 4 is more than 16 times the density of Group 1. This suggests that supermarkets have had limited success expanding into lower-income areas, their capacity to alleviate food insecurity constrained by their formalized nature, which makes them inaccessible to the lowest-income residents (Peyton et al 2015).

FIGURE 6: Target Consumer Base of South African Supermarket Chains

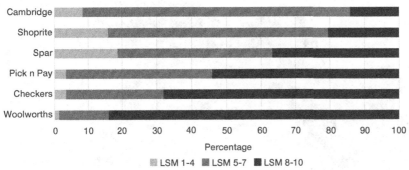

Source: Nortons Inc (2016)

Determined attempts are being made by large-scale food retailers in South Africa to draw in lower-income consumers. Shoprite-owned Usave, for example, is a supermarket brand that stocks low-price bulk goods and was developed for the purpose of targeting poor communities. Peyton et al (2015) mapped the distribution of Usave outlets in Cape Town and found that their distribution differed markedly from that of supermarkets in general (Figure 8). Usave outlets are disproportionately located in the lower-income Cape Flats area, rather than the higher-income suburbs and CBD. To date, their distribution in low-income areas has been limited mainly to the edges of the Cape Flats region, which "has provided many in lower income neighbourhoods with a cheaper alternative food source, but it has neglected those most in need; those in the central Cape Flats region, where poverty is most heavily concentrated" (Peyton et al 2015).

A growing trend in South Africa is what Battersby (2017) calls the mallification of South Africa's food retail environment. Nationally, the number of shopping malls increased from 1,053 in 2007 to 1,942 in 2015. An increasing number of new supermarkets in South Africa are not stand-alone stores but the main tenants in shopping malls. One of the issues being investigated by the South African Competition Commission is collusion between mall owners and supermarket chains to keep other supermarket chains out of malls. Most malls also have fast food courts or outlets, some of which (such as Hungry Lion) are owned by the supermarket chain. The process of mallification can also be seen outside South Africa including in Windhoek in Namibia.

FIGURE 7: Supermarket Distribution in Cape Town

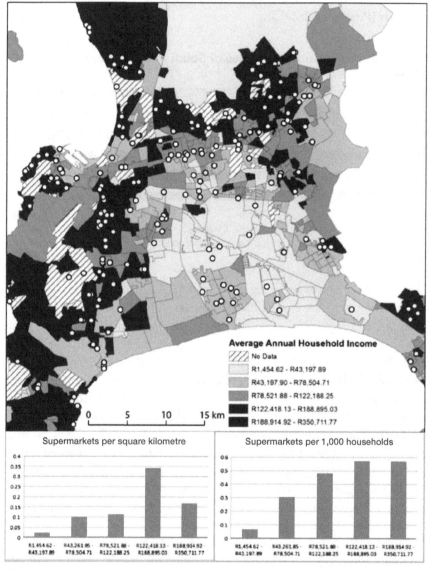

Source: Peyton et al. (2015)

FIGURE 8: Usave Distribution in Cape Town

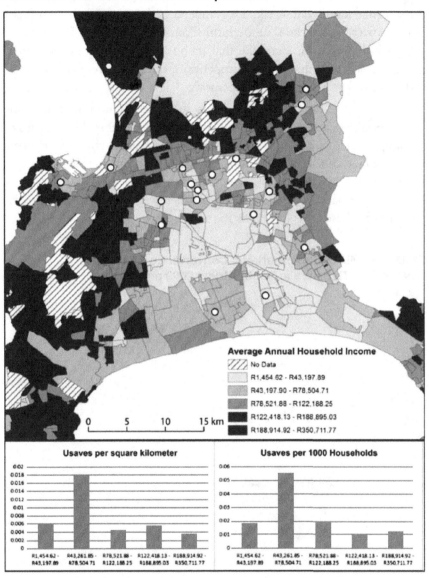

Source: Peyton et al. (2015)

3.3 Supermarkets and Informal Food Vendors

The impact of supermarket expansion on the informal food economy is now a subject of investigation by the South African Competition Commission's Retail Market Inquiry (Cheadle 2017). Between 2009 and 2015, the number of independent retailers across South Africa grew from 93,000 to 140,000 (a 45% increase) (Figure 9). The number of supermarkets (including hypermarkets) increased by 26% over the same period, and the number of convenience stores by 17%. These numbers might suggest that supermarket expansion is not having a negative impact on the informal food retail sector. That, indeed, is the argument of corporate South Africa before the Competition Commission. Pick n Pay's public submission asserts, for example, that its business activities do not "give rise to a material reduction in competition, or to any prejudice to small and independent retailers." Furthermore:

> The introduction of supermarkets in these communities has not materially negatively affected small, informal businesses such as spaza shops. There are only a limited number of studies which have been conducted in this regard and their findings do not appear to support any definitive conclusions that the introduction of shopping centres and supermarkets are the direct cause of any potential decline in spaza shops in these areas (Nortons Inc 2017).

FIGURE 9: Mix of Supermarkets, Convenience Stores and Independent Retailers in South Africa, 2009 and 2015

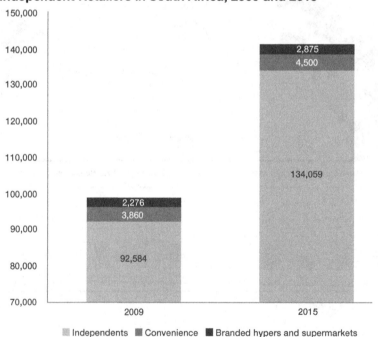

Source: Nortons Inc (2017)

Such corporate self-justification contrasts sharply with a submission from a consortium of research organizations which argues that:

> By actively facilitating development of shopping malls in the vicinity of the township, yet making no allowance for informal business, local government and big business form a highly effective partnership to outcompete and dominate over the township retail grocery sector (Petersen 2017).

Skinner and Haysom (2017) argue that the South African evidence is mixed on the impact of supermarket expansion on the informal food sector because it is context dependent. A review of the research literature on Southern Africa found a complex and nuanced picture, even in South Africa where supermarkets command a major share of food retail and the informal food sector is of comparatively recent origin (Crush and Frayne, 2011b). In some cities, such as Msunduzi, the food sector is completely dominated by supermarkets (Crush and Caesar 2016). The balance sheet on the impact of shopping mall development on small township retailers in Johannesburg suggests a decline in informal market share. In Cape Town, there is evidence to suggest a strong and co-dependent relationship between street traders and the formal food system (Battersby et al 2017). Recent research points to the vibrancy and resilience of the informal food economy, as well as its many points of intersection with the formal sector (Battersby and Peyton 2014, Battersby et al 2017, Peyton et al 2015).

Outside South Africa, the informal food economy co-exists with supermarkets, even in cities where the urban food supply is increasingly controlled by corporate supply chains. On the basis of work in Lusaka, Abrahams (2009, 2011) suggests that the impact of supermarkets in Zambia has been exaggerated and that the local food supply chains persist. In cities where supermarket penetration is very recent, the informal food economy does appear to be more robust as a food source for the urban poor (Crush and Frayne 2011b):

> Although supermarket penetration is very uneven at present, the question is whether other countries will follow trends already documented in South Africa…and what the impact will be on the informal food economy. One general conclusion from the Zambian case seems to be that the informal economy remains extremely vibrant and will not be significantly impacted by modern supply chains orchestrated by South African supermarket firms. In Southern Africa as a whole, informal markets, informal traders and street foods continue to play a critical role in food provisioning. In 2006, for example, informal traders still accounted for more than 90 per cent of the market share of fresh fruit and vegetables marketed in most low-income SADC countries. However, it would be premature to conclude that Southern Africa's supermarket revolution will therefore not radically transform urban food supply systems in countries outside South Africa in the future (Crush and Frayne 2011b).

Research by AFSUN found that while 79% of low-income households across Southern Africa purchased food at supermarkets, the informal food sector was also patronized by 70% of households. However, there was a considerable degree of inter-city variation in the relative importance of these two sources of food (Table 4). The data seems to suggest that there are three types of scenario:

- South African cities with extremely high patronage of the supermarket sector and variable use of the informal sector;
- Cities in countries neighbouring South Africa with extremely high supermarket patronage and much lower patronage of the informal food sector; and
- Cities in more distant countries with low supermarket usage and high levels of patronage of the informal sector.

The Windhoek picture was most similar to Cape Town, with very high supermarket use (97%) but significant, though not as high, purchasing from informal vendors (76%). The question, then, is whether the co-existence model identified for Cape Town is also at work in Windhoek or whether the proportion of households shopping at informal sites has declined since the AFSUN survey in 2008.

TABLE 4: Supermarkets and the Informal Sector in Southern African Cities, 2008		
City	Supermarkets (% of households)	Informal vendors (% of households)
South Africa		
Msunduzi	97	42
Johannesburg	96	85
Cape Town	94	66
Other Southern Africa		
Gaborone, Botswana	97	29
Windhoek, Namibia	97	76
Manzini, Swaziland	90	48
Maseru, Lesotho	84	49
Blantyre, Malawi	53	99
Harare, Zimbabwe	30	98
Maputo, Mozambique	23	98
Lusaka, Zambia	16	100
Source: AFSUN		

4. SOUTH AFRICAN SUPERMARKETS IN AFRICA

4.1 Corporate Expansion

Since the end of apartheid, South African companies have rapidly expanded into the rest of Africa. The penetration of supermarkets is thus part of a broader process of corporate profit-seeking. As Figure 10 shows, the main sectors (in terms of the number of countries with South African operations) include chemicals, tourism, construction, ICT, telecoms and transportation. Retailers (which include supermarket chains) are next, with a presence in 17 countries. Fast food/restaurant companies are in 15 countries. The spatial distribution of investment varies considerably (Figure 11). South Africa's corporate footprint in Africa is heaviest in the countries of the Southern African Development Community (SADC). With the exception of Angola and the DRC, over 40 South African companies operate in each SADC country. Botswana, Swaziland and Namibia each have more than 50 South African companies. Namibia is thus one of the major target countries for South African corporate expansion.

FIGURE 10: South African Companies in Other African Countries by Sector

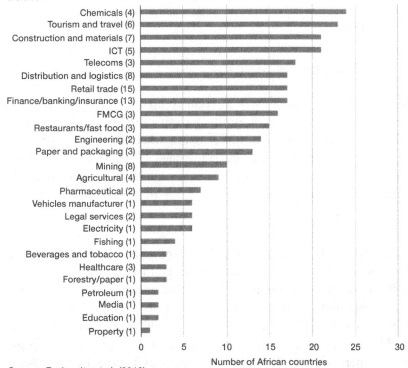

Source: Berkowitz et al. (2012)

FIGURE 11: South African Companies in Rest of Africa

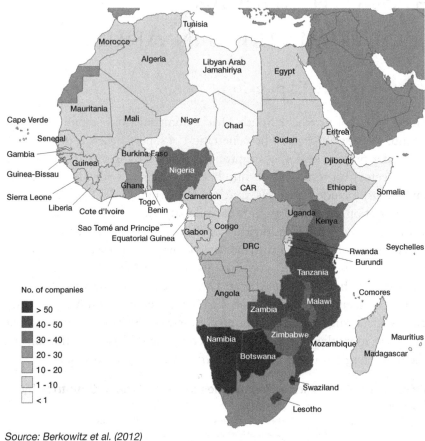

Source: Berkowitz et al. (2012)

4.2 South Africa's Supermarkets

Deloitte (2015) lists Africa's top 25 retail companies by revenue earned (Table 5). The top five are all South African supermarket chains. The growing power and control of these supermarket chains over the food system in South Africa has been accompanied by simultaneous expansion in other African countries (Dakora et al. 2010). Their presence is particularly strong in Southern Africa but they are also expanding in East, Central, and West Africa.

4.2.1 Shoprite Holdings Ltd. (das Nair and Dube, 2017; Shoprite, 2016): The Shoprite Group is South Africa and Africa's largest food retailer (by store number) and, as of 2016, operated 1,514 corporate supermarket, hypermarket, and convenience outlets in 15 countries across the continent. Another 123 new locations across all formats were set to be opened by the end of 2017. The retail formats and store brands comprise Shoprite supermarkets, Checkers supermarkets, Checkers hypers, Usave and OK Food stores as well as distribution centres, OK Furniture outlets, OK Power Express stores, House & Home stores, and Hungry Lion fast food outlets. The company is publicly listed on the Johannesburg Stock Exchange (JSE) Ltd, with secondary listings on both the Namibian and Zambian Stock Exchanges. The company's total assets grew from ZAR18 billion in 2010 to nearly ZAR50 billion in 2016 (Figure 12). Annual reports suggest that the Shoprite Group has a broad customer base that closely mirrors the demographic profile of each country in which they operate. Data presented by Nortons Inc (2016) challenges this notion, however (Figure 6). Checkers tends to focus exclusively on high-income markets while the Usave supermarket format targets the lower end of the market. Shoprite also owns the OK Franchise Division, which includes OK Foods, OK MiniMark, OK Express and OK Grocer.

TABLE 5: Africa's Major Retail Companies, 2013				
Retail Revenue Rank FY13	Name of company	Head-quarter country	Core retail segment 2013	FY13 revenue (USD million)
1	Shoprite Holdings Ltd	South Africa	Food and beverage	9,852.5
2	Massmart Holdings Ltd	South Africa	General goods	7,529.9
3	Pick n Pay Stores Ltd	South Africa	Food and beverage	6,343.3
4	Spar Group Ltd	South Africa	Food and beverage	5,166.7
5	Woolworths Holdings Ltd	South Africa	Clothing and accessories	3,827.8
6	Foschini Group Ltd	South Africa	Clothing and accessories	1,594.1
7	Mr Price Group Ltd	South Africa	Clothing and accessories	1,557.7
8	Clicks Group Ltd	South Africa	Health and personal care	1,349.7
9	JD Group Ltd (Steinhoff Holdings)	South Africa	Furniture	1,141.3
10	Truworths International Ltd	South Africa	Clothing and accessories	1,008.2
11	Label'Vie SA	Morocco	General goods	681.9
12	Choppies Enterprises Ltd	Botswana	Food and beverage	567.9
13	Lewis Group Ltd	South Africa	Electronics/appliances	523.4
14	OK Zimbabwe Ltd	Zimbabwe	Food and beverage	483.7
15	Iliad Africa Ltd	South Africa	Building materials	464.2
16	Société Magasin Général SA	Tunisia	General goods	454.5
17	PZ Cussons Nigeria Plc	Nigeria	Electronics/appliances	444.7
18	Meikles Ltd	Zimbabwe	Food and beverage	346.4
19	Sefalana Holding Co Ltd	Botswana	General goods	229.6
20	Zambeef Products Plc	Zambia	Food and beverage	171.8

21	Uchumi Supermarkets Ltd	Kenya	Food and beverage	163.8
22	AVI Ltd	South Africa	Food and beverage	155.7
23	Fummart Ltd	South Africa	Furniture	131.6
24	Edgars Stores Ltd (Edcon)	Zimbabwe	Clothing and accessories	64.8
25	Rex Trueform Clothing Co Ltd	South Africa	Clothing and accessories	47.4

Source: Deloitte (2015: 9)

FIGURE 12: Shoprite Total Assets, 2010-2016

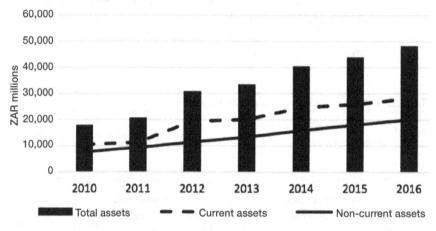

Source: das Nair and Dube (2017)

TABLE 6: Shoprite in Africa, 2015								
	Shoprite	Checkers	Checkers Hyper	Usave	OK Furniture	OK Franchise Division	House & Home	Hungry Lion
South Africa	400	180	31	266	255	183	45	124
Angola	7			14	5			7
Botswana	5	1		5	7		1	9
DRC	1							1
Ghana	3			1				
Lesotho	5			6	6	1		3
Madagascar	8							
Malawi	3			3				
Mauritius	3							
Mozambique	8			3	5			
Namibia	18	4		23	11	18	2	11
Nigeria	10							
Swaziland	9			5	4	4		1
Uganda	3							
Zambia	20			1	2			11
Total	503	185	31	327	295	206	48	167

Source: Based on Dakora (2016: 12) and company websites

As Table 6 shows, Shoprite's presence is massively weighted towards the South African market. In 2015, however, it had a presence in 14 other African countries which included 103 Shoprite supermarkets, 5 Checkers supermarkets (with 4 in Windhoek, Namibia), 61 Usave supermarkets and 21 OK outlets. Its Hungry Lion fast-food subsidiary had 23 outlets outside South Africa, including 11 in Namibia. Shoprite's presence is greatest in Southern Africa with a smaller footprint in countries such as Ghana and Nigeria.

4.2.2 Pick n Pay Stores Ltd. (das Nair and Dube 2017, Pick n Pay 2016): Pick n Pay is the second largest food retailer in Africa by revenue with head offices in Cape Town and Johannesburg. Through its subsidiaries and associates, the corporate entity in 2015 operated 235 supermarkets and hypermarkets in eight countries: South Africa, Botswana, Lesotho, Mauritius, Mozambique, Namibia, Swaziland and Zambia. The group, which attempts to cater to lower, middle and higher socio-economic communities, manages a variety of store formats, including hypermarkets, supermarkets, family franchise stores, mini market franchises, clothing stores, liquor stores, pharmacies, hardware stores and butcheries. It also owns a 49% share in TM Zimbabwe. In 2014, Pick n Pay had a market capitalization of ZAR35.5 billion. Its total assets increased from ZAR11 billion in 2010 to over ZAR16 billion in 2016 (Figure 13).

FIGURE 13: Pick n Pay Total Assets, 2010-2016

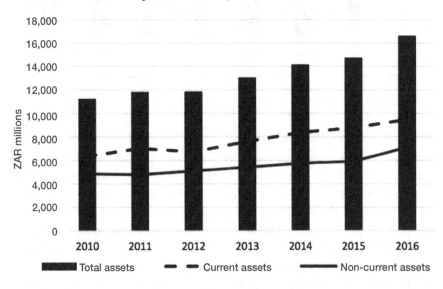

Source: das Nair and Dube (2017)

3.2.3 Spar Group South Africa Ltd. (das Nair and Dube 2017, Spar Group 2016): The Spar Group is the third largest food retailer in Africa by revenue and consists of Spar retailers, who are independent franchised store owners, and Spar Distribution Centres, which provide services for those retailers. Members pay a subscription to the group that is used for advertisements and promotions. Spar has aggressively expanded in Africa across a variety of retail formats, including supermarkets, convenience stores, hardware stores and liquor stores. The group has 944 SuperSpar and Spar outlets in 13 countries: South Africa, Angola, Botswana, Cameroon, Malawi, Mauritius, Mozambique, Namibia, Nigeria, Seychelles, Swaziland, Zambia and Zimbabwe. Its total assets increased from ZAR7.5 billion in 2010 to over ZAR25 billion in 2015 (Figure 14).

FIGURE 14: Spar Total Assets, 2010-2016

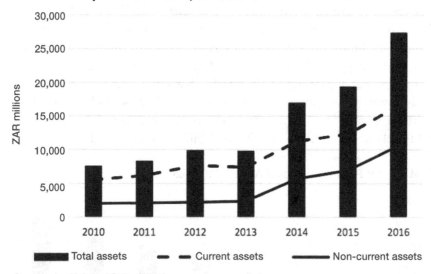

Source: das Nair and Dube (2017)

4.2.4 Woolworths Holdings (das Nair and Dube 2017, Woolworths 2016): While predominantly a clothing and accessories retailer, the group also sells food under its own brand name. Woolworths predominantly targets middle and upper socio-economic consumers. It also caters for consumers with an interest in high quality organic food products. The group has 397 food retailing outlets, mainly in shopping centres, in South Africa, Botswana, Ghana, Kenya, Lesotho, Mozambique, Namibia, Swaziland, Tanzania, Uganda and Zambia. Woolworths has also opened stand-alone food stores in convenient suburban locations. The total assets of the company increased from around ZAR9 billion in 2010 to nearly ZAR50 billion in 2016 (Figure 15).

FIGURE 15: Woolworths Total Assets, 2010-2016

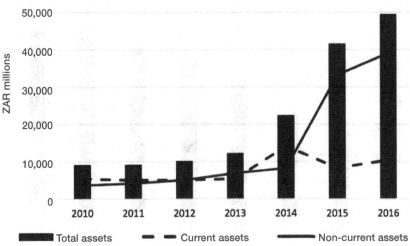

Source: das Nair and Dube (2017)

4.2.5 Fruit & Veg City Holdings (das Nair and Dube 2015, 2017): Fruit & Veg City is the fifth largest grocery retailer in terms of store numbers in South Africa. It started operations in Cape Town in 1993 and has expanded rapidly. There are now over 100 locations throughout Southern Africa. The chain has expanded into franchised convenience stores through a joint venture with fuel retail company Caltex. They have also introduced a fast food brand and diversified into the liquor market. Like other supermarkets, Fruit & Veg City now targets a broad demographic of customers, including through its Food Lover's Market format that focuses on wealthy suburbs. Unlike the other major supermarkets though, Fruit & Veg City focuses predominantly on the sale of fresh fruit and vegetables. The chain has outlets in South Africa, Lesotho, Mauritius, Namibia, Reunion, Tanzania, Zambia and Zimbabwe.

4.2.6 Massmart Holdings Ltd./Walmart (das Nair and Dube 2017): Massmart Holdings is a South African firm that was acquired by Walmart in 2011. The company owns a variety of retail formats including supermarket brands Game and Makro. Game has branched into food products, selling non-perishable groceries in its stores as well as basic foods wholesale as Game FoodCo. Walmart has indicated that it intends to expand Game FoodCo retail offerings considerably in South Africa (Greenberg 2017). Game has the advantage of Walmart's immense global supplier base, allowing it to benefit from lower unit costs. Massmart, which has outlets in South Africa, Botswana, Ghana, Kenya, Lesotho, Malawi, Mozambique, Namibia, Nigeria, Swaziland, Tanzania, Uganda and Zambia, grew steadily between 2010 and 2016 (Figure 16).

FIGURE 16: Massmart Total Assets, 2010-2016

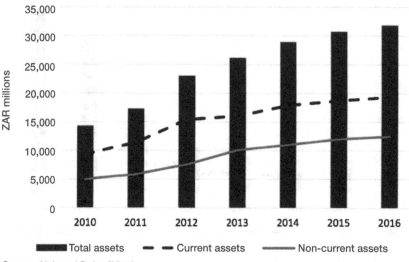

Source: Nair and Dube (2017)

The relative presence of different South African supermarkets varies from country to country. Compare, for example, Botswana, Zambia and Zimbabwe with South Africa (Figure 17). In South Africa, Shoprite, Pick n Pay and Spar are clearly dominant (with 88% of outlets). These companies have 78% of the outlets in Zambia, 57% in Zimbabwe and only 27% in Botswana (where local chain Choppies has 42% of the outlets).

There are numerous reasons why South African supermarkets have invested in the rest of Africa in the last two decades. First, the short and long term financial profits to be made by early entry into Africa's rapidly growing urban consumer markets are significant. *The Economist* argues that, as African economies expand, it is likely that food retailing will drive industry growth across the continent, with South African companies leading the way (Economist 2013). Second, Tschirley et al (2015) have traced the growth of an African middle-class with higher disposable incomes, changing dietary preferences, heavy expenditure on processed food, and a taste preference for food purchase at modern retail outlets. Third, in the context of high rates of formal-sector unemployment, there is a readily available and cheap labour force to utilize in supermarket and value chain operations. Fourth, the accessibility of supermarkets to South African producers and suppliers has played a significant role in creating regional supply chains and increasing capacity for expansion. South African companies can use their already established procurement networks in South Africa to penetrate other urbanizing markets within the region and continent. Finally, supermarket supply chains achieve major economies of scale when compared to the long, inefficient, and informal food supply chain systems that have historically dominated African food markets.

FIGURE 17: Supermarket Presence in Botswana, South Africa, Zambia and Zimbabwe

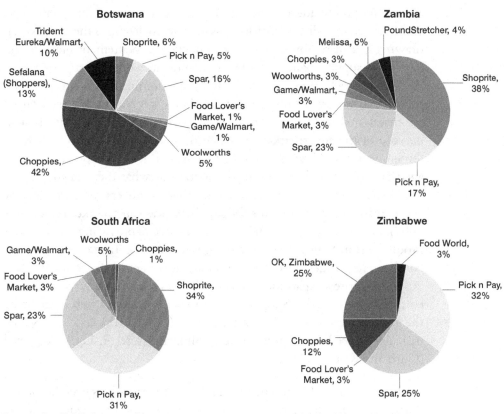

Source: das Nair (nd)

South African supermarkets have encountered various obstacles in different regions of the continent, particularly those further from South Africa. Dakora et al (2010), for example, found that cross-national systems connectivity, low development levels of local production and supply, labour disputes, land issues in managing franchisees, complex international supply chains, import duties, and domestic competition all present challenges for food retail expansion. They categorize the barriers in supply chain expansion as "hard" or "soft." Hard barriers relate to physical infrastructure and utilities. Roads, railways, ports, airports and electricity are the main delivery systems for retail companies to get their goods to market, yet this infrastructure is inadequate in many African economies. Soft barriers comprise the bureaucratic environment of government legislation on imports and exports, and regional and international bilateral/multilateral trade and customs agreements. Other soft barriers are land tenure rights issues, non-uniformity in regulations and market structures for freight/cargo, protectionist policies of African governments, and different geopolitical climates and dynamics with volatile and fragmented markets (Dakora et al 2016).

4.3 Supermarkets in Question

While the proliferation of South African supermarkets throughout the continent is an indication of food system formalization, the process has drawn a mixed response due to the effects of procurement practices on local food supply chains and the labour practices of some supermarkets. Abrahams (2009) notes efforts to discipline dominant supermarkets and their exclusionary sourcing practices. For example, in Nigeria, farmers threatened to burn down a South African-owned Shoprite branch because of the supermarket's practice of procuring food products from foreign sources (Abrahams 2009). In Uganda, local authorities encouraged farmers to seek government support for what they called "invading" supermarket supply chains by helping producers meet the quality and consistency requirements for supplying the supermarket (Abrahams 2009). Furthermore, Shoprite's alleged practice of procuring 80% of their products from South Africa led the government of Tanzania to publicly condemn its practices prior to their selling their assets in the country (Ciuri 2013). Shoprite's expansion in East Africa has also been thwarted by local competition. In 2014, Shoprite's locations in Tanzania were bought by the growing Kenyan retail giant Nakumatt (Ciuri 2013). In 2015, Nakumatt announced its intention to buy Shoprite stores in Uganda as well (Ciuri and Kisembo 2015).

As the internationalization of South African supermarkets stretches across Africa, and specifically into Namibia, more attention is needed to assess with evidence the risks and benefits this poses for local food supply chains and the food security of urban households. Issues that need examination in Namibia and other countries with a growing supermarket presence include:

- The structure of the supply chains of supermarkets and whether local producers (including rural smallholders), processors and transporters are integrated into those chains and, if they are, what types of benefits they derive. The related question is whether supermarkets source any of their products from local (Namibian) suppliers and how much they import from South Africa and who benefits most.

- The relationship between supermarkets and informal food retailers (and their livelihoods) and whether the growing presence of supermarkets inhibits or stimulates the informal food economy. The informal food economy has historically played an essential role in the supply of fresh and perishable food products to the urban poor in African cities. However, this may be changing. A case study conducted in Lusaka, Zambia, by Abrahams (2009) showed that informal food markets present a considerable challenge to the claims that supermarkets transform food economies in urban Africa. In South Africa, the evidence is mixed on whether supermarkets inhibit the development of informal food entrepreneurship (Crush and Frayne 2011a, Skinner and Haysom 2017). The relationship between supermarkets and the informal food retail sector in Namibia is largely unexplored.

- Previous research in Namibia has highlighted the high levels of food insecurity in Windhoek (Kazembe and Nickanor 2014, Nickanor 2014, Pendleton et al 2014). The growing presence of modern food retailing in Southern Africa has implications for food environments and the food security of the urban poor. The process of supermarkets initially locating in high-income neighbourhoods means that accessibility for urban dwellers in poor neighbourhoods is limited by factors such as distance, means of transportation, and associated monetary costs. Supermarkets in South Africa are attempting to expand their customer demographics from urban elites to include all urban consumers. Is this corporate strategy being replicated in other African countries, including Namibia, or are supermarkets outside South Africa still mainly serving middle and higher-income consumers and neighbourhoods?

- Supermarkets are potentially able to provide shoppers with a diverse diet, ranging from more expensive fresh and nutritious food products to less expensive energy-dense, nutrient-poor processed foods. In Botswana and Zambia, food prices are generally lower in supermarkets than in other food outlets, particularly for staples such as maize flour, bread, milk, rice and sugar. Conversely, while perishable food products in supermarkets are arguably safer and fresher than those in informal markets, their cost is often higher (Chidozie et al 2014). The key question here, given the well-established inverse relationship between household income and the proportion of income spent on food, is whether supermarkets make food more affordable and whether they provide for a more diverse and nutritious diet.

- In African cities, obesity and associated NCDs are a new dimension of food insecurity and a growing public health concern (Hawkes 2008). In South Africa, public health researchers have pointed a finger at "Big Food" for providing cheap and accessible highly refined fats, oils, sugars and carbohydrates (Igumbor et al 2011). Diets consisting of high-sugar and high-fat food products are reaching epidemic proportions and South African supermarkets are being held partially responsible. The growth in number of supermarkets in Namibia indicates an urgent need to research a possible nutrition transition and the implications for public health.

- The policy implications of the spread and increase in power of supermarkets are poorly understood and extend across different levels of governance. Interventions by governments designed to protect local producers and manufacturers by, for example, banning the imports of certain products, imposing import tariffs and setting quotas for local procurement, can affect supermarket cross-border supply chains. Similarly, as the South African case suggests, governments may intervene to try to ensure fair competition in the supermarket sector and between the sector and informal retailers and vendors. This raises the question of municipal attitudes towards informality and whether they provide an enabling or hostile environment for informal food vendors.

5. STUDY METHODOLOGY

The research programme for this study was funded by the Open Society Foundation for South Africa and conducted by the Department of Statistics and Population Studies (University of Namibia), in partnership with the African Food Security Urban Network (AFSUN), the Hungry Cities Partnership (HCP) and the Balsillie School of International Affairs (BSIA). The research programme had five main components:

- Mapping of Food Retail Outlets: The spatial mapping of supermarkets and open markets in Windhoek was undertaken by researchers at the Department of Statistics and Population Studies at the University of Namibia. The addresses of outlets were plotted on city maps by name and address and then reduced to scale using GIS.

- Supermarket Supply Chains: Several supermarket managers were approached about sharing their product inventories but were not able to do so. A novel methodology was therefore used to compile inventories in two supermarkets (a Checkers and a Shoprite). With the permission of store managers, students used their cellphones to photograph products on supermarket shelves to record product type, brand name, quantity and source country. The information on the photographs was then extracted and recorded on Excel spreadsheets for analysis. Many products did not show a country of origin. Others could be inferred (for example, many fruit and vegetable products were labelled with the Freshmark brand which signifies import from South Africa). The primary purpose of this exercise was to understand the relative importance of imported versus locally-produced/processed foodstuffs and to begin to understand to what extent supermarket supply chains were within country, bilateral (South Africa-Namibia), regional or international.

- Household Food Security and Supermarket Patronage: A total of 875 Windhoek households were interviewed using the AFSUN-HCP Household Food Security Baseline Survey, which collects a wide range of demographic, economic and food consumption and sourcing data at the household level. Households surveyed in the 10 constituencies of Windhoek were identified using a two-stage sampling design. As a first step, primary sampling units (PSUs) were randomly selected with probability proportional to size. The PSUs were selected from a master frame developed and demarcated for the 2011 Population and Housing Census. Within the 10 constituencies, a total of 35 PSUs were selected covering the whole of Windhoek, and 25 households were systematically selected in each PSU. The sampled PSUs and households were located on maps, which were used to target households for interviews. Table 7 summarizes the number of PSUs identified in each constituency and the corresponding household and population sizes. The survey was implemented using tablet technology.

- In-Depth Interviews: The interviews were conducted in two phases. In the first phase, 36 key informant interviews were conducted. The constituency councillors where the household survey took place were asked to provide the names of people from their respective constituencies who were knowledgeable about the socio-economic, poverty, employment and food security situation in those constituencies. The selection of the informants was stratified by gender, employment status, age and income categories. In the second phase, 20 food vendors were interviewed. They were chosen to represent a variety of operating locations, including selling from homes, open markets, major crossroad intersections and construction sites.

TABLE 7: Household Survey Sample				
Constituency	Selected PSU	Sampled households per PSU	Population in the sampled households	Population size in the sampled PSUs
John Pandeni	2	2 x 25	130	559
Katutura Central	2	2 x 25	151	726
Katutura East	2	2 x 25	149	733
Khomasdal	3	3 x 25	247	1,128
Moses Garoeb	6	6 x 25	543	1,648
Samora Machel	5	5 x 25	457	1,682
Tobias Hainyeko	5	5 x 25	372	1,231
Windhoek West	3	3 x 25	254	617
Windhoek East	6	6 x 25	520	1,814
Windhoek Rural	1	1 x 25	78	104
Total	35	875	2,901	10,242

6. SUPERMARKETS IN NAMIBIA AND WINDHOEK

6.1 Spatial Distribution of Supermarkets

All major South African supermarket chains have a presence in Namibia, with Shoprite, Pick n Pay and Spar being particularly prominent. Emongor (2008) used data from Planet Retail to rank the major supermarket chains in the country (Table 8). Of the nearly 160 supermarkets of which there is a record (i.e. the figure does not include local independent supermarkets), one-third are owned by Shoprite, followed by Pick n Pay (22%), Spar (18%) and Woolworths (4%) (Table 9). In Namibia, South African supermarkets face competition from a long-established local company with roots dating back to the 19th century. The Woermann Group is a family company controlled by descendants of early German settlers. It opened its first Woermann Brock (WB) supermarket in Windhoek in 1966 and now has nearly 30 WB supermarkets throughout the country (17% of the total). The group also has 13 wholesale Cash & Carry outlets around the country. Of the South African chains, Shoprite and Spar are the largest, followed by Pick n Pay, and predominantly sell food products. Woolworths has a presence but with limited food retailing.

TABLE 8: Top Supermarkets in Namibia, 2005					
	No. of stores	Sales area (m²)	Retail sales (EUR million)	% food sales	% non-food sales
Shoprite	48	46,300	131	72	28
Spar	23	14,000	18	90	10
Woermann Brock	15	-	-	90	10
Pick n Pay	9	7,200	28	90	10
Woolworths	5	4,000	9	5	95
Local independent	Many	350>	-	90	10
Source: Emongor (2009: 51)					

Data from current company reports suggests that both Shoprite and Spar have expanded their national presence in the last decade, but that Pick n Pay has grown the most (from 9 to 35 supermarkets). The advent of Massmart/Walmart and Fruit & Veg City is also noted (Table 9). Woermann Brock has experienced significant national growth (from 15 to 27 supermarkets). Windhoek itself, Namibia's major city and largest consumer market, has approximately 40 supermarkets (or a quarter of all supermarkets in the country). Of these, 22 (or nearly 60%) are South African-owned and 40% are Namibian-owned. Woermann Brock has six supermarkets in the city (16% of the total) and the other 10 (24%) are individually or family-owned. The Shoprite Group has the largest South African presence in the city with 12 supermarkets (including two Usaves, three Shoprites and five Checkers supermarkets). There are also four Spar, three Pick n Pay and three Fruit & Veg City outlets in the city.

TABLE 9: Number of Supermarkets in Namibia and Windhoek, 2016				
	Namibia		Windhoek	
	No.	%	No.	%
South African				
Shoprite	53	33.5	12	26.7
Pick n Pay	35	22.2	3	6.7
Spar	29	18.4	4	8.9
Woolworths	6	3.8	0	0.0
Massmart/Walmart	4	2.5	0	0.0
Fruit & Veg City	4	2.5	3	6.7
Namibian				
Woermann Brock	27	17.1	6	13.4
Other	-	-	17	37.6
Total	158	100.0	45	100.0
Source: Various company annual reports for 2016				

The geography of supermarkets in Windhoek has several distinctive features. First, the number of supermarkets varies considerably across the city with most concentrated in the higher-income areas of Windhoek East and Windhoek West. As Table 10 shows, 75% of the city's supermarkets are in these two constituencies. The number of supermarkets in lower-income areas is much lower and tends to be confined to locally owned supermarkets (including Woermann Brock) and Shoprite's Usave outlets. Other subsidiaries such as Shoprite and Checkers supermarkets are in higher-income areas of the city, as are competitors such as Pick n Pay supermarkets. Some Shoprite supermarkets, such as those in Montecristo and Katutura, are certainly relatively accessible to lower-income consumers. In general, however, there are no supermarkets in the sprawling and growing informal settlements to the north of the city. This might suggest that supermarkets are relatively inaccessible to the urban poor and that the informal food economy is stronger in these urban spaces. However, such a conclusion would be premature.

TABLE 10: Location of Supermarkets by Constituency			
	No. of supermarkets	No. of South African supermarkets	Poor/severely poor* %
Windhoek East	18	10	0.0
Windhoek West	12	9	0.0
John Pandeni	1	1	4.3

Katutura East	2	1	4.5
Katutura Central	2	1	8.3
Khomasdal	2	1	14.7
Samora Machel	2	0	37.5
Tobias Hainyeko	5	1	36.1
Moses Garoeb	1	0	77.8
Windhoek Rural	0	0	28.3
Total	45	24	100.0
*Based on 2016 NSA-NHIES poverty indicators			

FIGURE 18: Spatial Distribution of Supermarkets in Windhoek

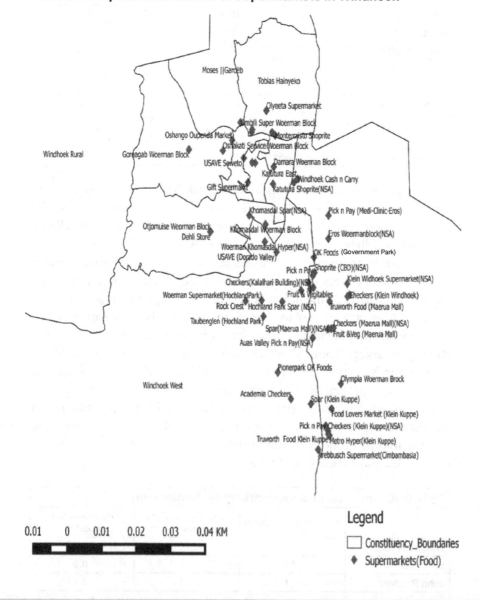

6.2 Supermarket Supply Chains

Detailed tracking of supermarket supply chains and analysis of procurement strategies was not possible given the privacy concerns expressed by supermarket managers. Emongor (2009) and Emongor and Kirsten (2009) were the first to provide insights into the distinctive nature of supermarket sourcing in a country in which (a) smallholder farming is largely confined to the north of the country, and (b) where the main city, Windhoek, is located in a relatively arid area with no large-scale horticultural production in the city-region. Emongor's (2009) census of the source of products on supermarket shelves showed the overwhelming domination of South Africa as a source of fresh food and vegetable products (Table 11). With regard to processed foods, South Africa was again dominant although all of the wheat and maize flour, pasta products and processed fresh milk brands were Namibian. However, with the exception of milk, the processing ingredients were mainly imported and processed by Namib Mills. Other findings (with updates where available) include the following:

- Some 80% of all processed foods sold in Namibia are imported from South Africa. The food and beverages processing sector in Namibia consists of three downstream sectors, namely meat processing contributing less than 10% to total manufacturing GDP, fish processing contributing 10-15% to total manufacturing GDP, and the manufacture of other foods and beverages contributing around half of total manufacturing GDP. There was only one dairy processor in Namibia, Namibia Dairies, and one milling company, Namib Mills. The food processing sector is therefore relatively small and although its products are found in Windhoek supermarkets, local production is insufficient to meet demand. At the same time, protectionist regulations mean that supermarkets procure most of their fresh milk from Namibia Diaries and their milled flour and pasta products from Namib Mills. Other dairy products, such as cheese and yoghurt, are imported from South Africa. According to Emongor (2008), there is a ban on the import of flour to Namibia so Namib Mills has a monopoly on the importation and processing of wheat and maize to flour.

- Emongor (2009) estimates that 82% of fresh fruit and vegetables come from South Africa and only 18% from Namibia. The imports come from South Africa through supply chains organized by subsidiaries such as Freshmark Namibia, Shoprite's fruit and vegetable procurement and distribution arm, and FreshCo (the Pick n Pay equivalent). Supermarkets are, however, required to source a certain percentage of their fresh produce from local farmers. According to Emongor (2009), Pick n Pay's FreshCo makes up this quota by sourcing from a single large-scale farmer in Okahandja. None of the Shoprite outlets buy directly from farmers in Namibia. FreshMark obtains some produce locally but mainly from large-scale farmers including watermelons from a farm at Etunda and tomatoes from two farms at Tsumeb. Fruit & Veg City procures cabbage, watermelons, pumpkins and tomatoes from two large farms in North Ruaka. Lettuce, cabbage and green peppers are also sourced from irrigated farms in Hardap and Okahandja. About 30% of vegetables are sourced locally, with the rest coming from fresh produce markets in Cape Town and Johannesburg (Emongor 2009). In a new venture started in 2014, Pick n Pay has been sourcing vegetables from an irrigated commercial farm at Otavifontein in the north of the country. These include cabbage, spinach, pumpkin, butternuts, potatoes, green peppers, broccoli and cauliflower (PnP 2017). The challenge of meeting quotas from local producers has led to charges that supermarkets are mislabelling products. In 2014, for example, the Namibian Standards Institution launched an inquiry into mislabelling practices by Freshmark, Shoprite and Checkers which were allegedly representing South African products as locally grown and produced (Kaira and Haidula 2014).

- Some large-scale farmers in Namibia who produce horticultural products such as onions and tomatoes under rain-fed conditions or limited irrigation opt to transport their produce to fresh produce markets in Johannesburg or Cape Town in South Africa, over 1,000km away. The farmers prefer these markets because they are easily accessible and farmers can sell large amounts of produce, reducing transaction and transportation costs (Emongor 2009: 50).

- Few small-scale farmers are integrated into supply chains. Emongor (2009) notes that apart from high transport costs, small-scale farmers are mainly involved in subsistence farming. Another constraint is inconsistent production implying that farmers cannot meet the year-round supply requirements. According to Freshmark Namibia, most small-scale producers are not able to meet the private grades and standards Freshmark demands. Lack of traceability and high transaction costs are some of the factors that contribute to Freshmark Namibia not procuring directly from small-scale farmers (Emongor 2009). According to the study, small-scale farmers are "automatically excluded" from the Shoprite supply chain in Namibia.

- Most of the red meat sold in supermarkets in Windhoek comes from within the country with supply chains that connect supermarkets with large-scale commercial ranching operations via MeatCo, the largest abattoir in the country. The commercial cattle farming area covers 14.5 million hectares in the northern half of the country. Cattle farming contributes 2-4% of Namibia's GDP and is practised by an estimated 2,250 farmers, with a combined average annual herd of

840,000. The total cattle herd is closer to 3 million as cattle are also raised by small farmers (Figure 19). Recent studies have highlighted the barriers facing small-scale cattle farmers from accessing formal markets (Thomas et al 2014, Kalundu and Meyer 2017). Around 300,000 cattle are marketed on average each year, roughly half as live cattle (almost exclusively as weaners) and half as beef. Almost all weaners are exported as live cattle to feed lots in South Africa. Around 55,000 tonnes of beef are produced per year and primarily sold to South African (45%) and international markets (40%) with around 15% consumed domestically (Figure 20) (Olbrich et al 2014: 4). In 2010, meat imports totalled 40,000 tonnes of which three-quarters were chicken (with the main sources being South Africa, Argentina, the US, Denmark and Brazil). The chicken industry in Namibia has increased dramatically since 2013 with the opening of a chicken meat production plant by Namib Poultry and an increase in small-scale chicken producers around the country (Figure 19) (Andjamba 2017).

TABLE 11: Source of Supermarket Products, 2008		
Products	Source	% of brands on shelves
Processed		
Frozen vegetables	South Africa	100
Fruit juices	South Africa	100
Canned vegetables	South Africa	100
Canned fruit	South Africa	100
Processed milk (UHT)	South Africa	100
Tomato sauces	South Africa/International	90/10
Wheat and maize flour	Namibia	100
Pasta products	Namibia	100
Processed fresh milk	Namibia	100
Fresh vegetables		
Carrots	South Africa	100
Irish potatoes	South Africa	100
Cabbages	South Africa	100
Onions	South Africa	100
Leafy vegetables	South Africa/Namibia	90/10
Tomatoes	South Africa/Namibia	90/10
Fresh fruit		
Apples	South Africa	100
Oranges	South Africa	100
Bananas	South Africa	100
Mangoes	South Africa	100
Source: Emongor (2009)		

FIGURE 19: Livestock Population in Namibia, 2009-2015

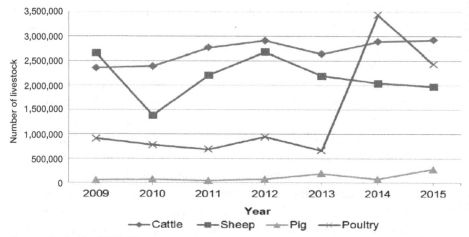

Source: Andjamba (2017: 21)

FIGURE 20: Beef Production, Trade and Consumption in Namibia, 2007-2012

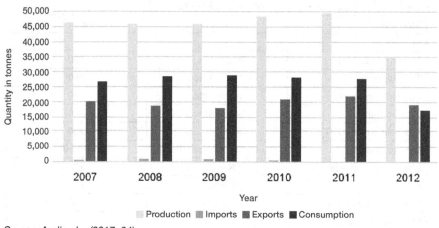

Source: Andjamba (2017: 24)

Ijuma et al (2015) argue that the rise in consumption of processed food in East and Southern Africa has been "deep", accounting for nearly 70% of purchased food. Their analysis of the processed food sector in Tanzania found that local and regional food processing was very competitive with imports from outside East Africa and was characterized by the rise of a few medium and large processors and "a surge of many micro and small firms" producing branded but largely undifferentiated meal and flour. They found that of 953 products, 564 (59%) were manufactured within Tanzania, 113 (12%) were from neighbouring countries (Kenya and Uganda) and 256 (29%) were sourced internationally. This study, the only one of its kind in Africa, provides a baseline for comparison with the product data collected at two Shoprite-owned supermarkets in Windhoek.

In sharp contrast to Tanzania, where 59% of processed products are manufactured in the country, in the Windhoek study of Shoprite outlets, only 25% of products were manufactured in-country and 8% were from outside Africa. This means that 67% of products were manufactured in South Africa and imported. There are only three product categories – cereals and cereal products, dairy products and processed meat – where there are more local than imported products in Windhoek. In all other categories, there are more imported than locally produced products. As Table 12 suggests, Shoprite's supply chains for processed foods are dominated by imports from South Africa. As many as two-thirds of the processed products come from South Africa and that country has an almost complete monopoly on canned food, sauces, spreads, desserts and frozen foods. Its high number of cereal products is related to its domination of the supply of breakfast cereals. It also has a commanding presence in the soft drinks (including fruit juices and pop), condiments (including tea and coffee) and snacks categories. What is perhaps surprising is how little sourcing Shoprite appears to do within the region (with canned pineapples from Swaziland and orange juice concentrate from Zimbabwe the only recorded products). Equally, Europe and Asia are only sources for certain specialized foods. Thailand is the main source of rice. One oddity is that Thai rice is imported directly into the country by Namib Mills and also comes in via South African manufacturers. Packaged rice from both sources can be found on the same supermarket shelves. Many of the European and Asian products may also be imported via South Africa. The only US product of the 642 sold is tabasco sauce.

TABLE 12: Source of Processed Foods in Checkers and Shoprite, Windhoek

Product category	Total no. of products	Namibia	South Africa	Other SADC	Europe	Asia	Other
Cereals incl. foods from cereals	136	68	51	0	6	11	1
Soft drinks	112	19	92	1	0	0	0
Snacks	108	30	71	0	3	3	1
Canned food	79	3	54	1	15	4	2
Sauces	43	0	39	0	0	4	0
Condiments	41	6	33	0	0	2	0
Spreads	31	0	23	0	4	2	2
Dairy	29	22	7	0	0	0	0
Desserts	24	0	24	0	0	0	0
Frozen foods	23	0	23	0	0	0	0
Meats	16	13	3	0	0	0	0
Total	642	161	419	2	28	26	6
%	100.0	25.1	65.3	0.3	4.4	4.0	0.9

7. POVERTY AND FOOD INSECURITY IN WINDHOEK

7.1 The Geography of Poverty

According to the 2016 poverty indicators of the Namibia Statistics Agency's Namibia Household Income and Expenditure Survey (NSA-NHIES), households that spent less than NAD520.80 per month on basic necessities were classified as poor (the upper bound poverty line or UBPL) and those that spent less than NAD389.30 per month were considered severely poor (the lower bound poverty line or LBPL). Using the net household income survey data for the month preceding the survey, and the NSA-NHIES poverty lines, we calculated that 13% of the surveyed households were poor and 9% were severely poor (Table 13). However, about one-fifth (21%) of households in informal settlements were severely poor, while close to one-third (29%) were classified as poor. Severe poverty tended to increase with household size (with the exception of households with six or more members), while poverty levels decreased with increasing size. This may be because in poor households the probability of having more than one adult earner increases with size, while in severely poor households a single income may have to support more people. Levels of poverty and severe poverty were highest in female-centred households. According to the National Planning Commission (NPC nd: 33), within Windhoek severe poverty is found in the Tobias Hainyeko, Moses Garoeb and Windhoek Rural constituencies and increased in all constituencies between 2001 and 2011, except in Windhoek East and Windhoek West (Figure 21).

In terms of the spatial distribution of income poverty, the survey showed that Moses Garoeb had the highest levels of both poor (35% of the total) and severely poor (43% of the total) households (Table 14). By contrast, the higher-income areas of Windhoek West and Windhoek East did not have any poor or severely poor households.

FIGURE 21: Change in Poverty Headcount Rate, 2001-2011

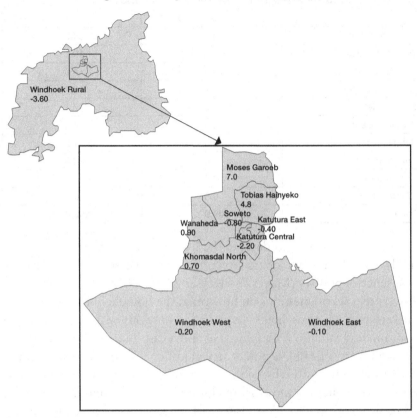

Source: NPC (nd: 33)

TABLE 13: Income Poverty Levels and Household Characteristics			
	% of total households	Income poverty	
		Severely poor	Poor
Housing			
Formal	44.1	0.7	2.6
Informal	55.9	20.6	28.6
Household size			
1 member	8.8	8.8	17.6
2-3 members	29.8	17.7	23.7
4-5 members	31.9	11.1	14.1
6 or more members	29.5	9.0	14.0
Household structure			
Female-centred	32.4	15.0	22.1
Male-centred	18.9	11.0	14.2
Nuclear	23.6	14.7	20.0
Extended	23.1	5.6	8.8

TABLE 14: Income Poverty Levels by Constituency		
	Severely poor %	Poor %
Moses Garoeb	43.0	34.8
Tobias Hainyeko	16.5	19.6
Windhoek Rural	13.9	14.3
Samora Machel	12.7	13.4
Khomasdal	7.6	7.1
Katutura Central	3.8	4.5
John Pandeni	2.5	1.8
Windhoek East	0.0	0.0
Katutura East	0.0	4.5
Windhoek West	0.0	0.0
Total	100.0	100.0

The survey also collected data on the lived poverty index (LPI), a commonly used barometer of quality of life that measures the subjective experience of poverty (Meyer and Keyser 2016). The LPI is derived from answers to a set of questions on how often the household has gone without certain basic households items in the previous year. These include food, medical attention, cooking fuel and a cash income. The responses are on a Likert scale of five points: never; just once or twice; several times; many times; and always. From the Likert scale, a mean LPI score is computed for each item: a mean score closer to 0 indicates fewer households 'going without', while a score closer to 4 suggests more households 'going without'.

The mean score for the entire sample was 1.78. Eighteen percent of households had an LPI of 2.01–3.00; and 5% a score of 3.01–4.00. As with income poverty, there were striking differences in LPI scores within Windhoek, with households in Windhoek East, Windhoek West and John Pandeni constituencies having 100% or close to 100% of households lacking no basic household needs (LPI of 1.00 or below). Comparatively, in Tobias Hainyeko, Katutura East, Moses Garoeb and Samora Machel constituencies, only about 30%–50% of the households had an LPI of 1.00 or less. In these areas, Katutura East had the highest percentage (16%) with LPI scores of 3.01–4.00, compared to Samora Machel (7%), Tobias Hainyeko (5%) and Moses Garoeb (4%).

FIGURE 22: Lived Poverty Index by Constituency

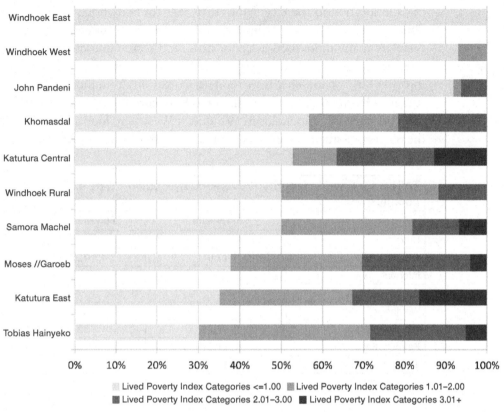

7.2 Levels of Food Insecurity in Windhoek

There is a vigorous international debate about how best to quantify levels of food insecurity in a population (Coates 2013). The AFSUN-HCP Household Food Security Baseline Survey uses four measures of food security developed and recommended by the Food and Nutrition Technical Assistance (FANTA) project. In this report we use three of these measures to assess the prevalence of food insecurity in Windhoek: (a) the Household Food Insecurity Access Score (HFIAS), a continuous score between 0 (completely food secure) and 27 (completely food insecure) based on nine frequency of occurrence questions; (b) the HFIAS frequency of occurrence questions are grouped into four categories (food secure, mildly food secure, moderately food insecure and severely food insecure) as the Household Food Insecurity Access Prevalence (HFIAP) classification; and (c) the Household Dietary Diversity Score (HDDS) which captures the household diet profile in the previous 24 hours in terms of the number of food groups (from 0 to 12) from which foods were consumed.

The HFIAP shows that food insecurity varies both with type of housing and location in the city. More than 90% of households in informal housing structures are food insecure (Table 15). In most constituencies, there are many more food insecure than food secure households. In the low-income areas of the city with a high concentration of informal housing, over 80% of households are food insecure. Only Windhoek East constituency has more food secure than food insecure households, although 48% of surveyed households in Windhoek West were food secure. In all the other constituencies, over 75% of households classify as food insecure.

TABLE 15: Food Insecurity Prevalence by Housing Type and Location		
	Food secure %	Food insecure %
Housing		
Formal	27.6	72.4
Informal	8.0	92.0
Constituency		
Windhoek East	72.7	27.3
Windhoek West	47.7	52.3
Katutura East	21.3	78.7
John Pandeni	16.9	83.1
Samora Machel	16.1	83.9
Khomasdal	14.0	86.0
Tobias Hainyeko	11.1	88.9
Moses Garoeb	10.8	89.2
Katutura Central	9.6	90.4
Windhoek Rural	8.1	91.9

The Household Dietary Diversity Score measures another aspect of food security, i.e. the quality of the household diet. A low score (out of 12) means a narrow and monotonous diet, whereas a high score indicates a more diverse and healthier pattern of food consumption. The mean HDDS for all surveyed households was an extremely low 3.21 (out of 12). This indicates that most households had consumed food from fewer than four food groups in the previous 24 hours. Figure 23 shows that there is a strong association between lived poverty and dietary diversity. As the LPI score increases, dietary diversity decreases. Households with an LPI over 2.0 had a mean HDDS of less than 2, while those with a lower LPI had a higher HDDS.

A lack of diversity in the diet was closely related to the level of household food security (as measured by the HFIAP). Food insecure households had a mean HDDS of 2.95 while food secure households had a mean HDDS of 4.47. Additional insights are gained by cross-tabulating the HDDS and HFIAP by type of housing (Table 16). Households in formal housing had a more diverse diet than those in informal housing (3.88 versus 2.66). Households in formal areas had higher HDDS scores than those in informal areas in both food secure (4.72 versus 3.78) and food insecure (3.56 versus 2.56) households. Further, food secure households in informal areas had a higher HDDS than food insecure households in formal areas (3.78 versus 3.56).

FIGURE 23: Household Dietary Diversity and Lived Poverty

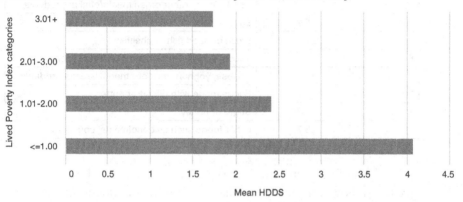

TABLE 16: Dietary Diversity by Food Insecurity and Type of Housing

Food insecurity prevalence	Housing type	Mean	No.
Food secure	Formal housing	4.72	103
	Informal housing	3.78	37
	Total	4.47	140
Food insecure	Formal housing	3.56	268
	Informal housing	2.56	433
	Total	2.95	701
Total	Formal housing	3.88	371
	Informal housing	2.66	470
	Total	3.20	841

Another way of looking at consumption patterns is the raw data on food group choice. Virtually all households consumed products from Food Group No. 1 (cereals) (Table 17). The second most commonly consumed were foodstuffs from No. 5 (meat and meat products), consumed by nearly 50% of households, followed by No. 11 (sugar) by around a third of households. Around 30% of households consumed oil products (mainly cooking oil) but only 20% consumed vegetables and fish. Dairy products were consumed by less than 15% and fruit by less than 10%.

TABLE 17: Level of Household Consumption from Each Food Group		
Food group	% of households	Types of food
1	95.0	Pasta, bread, rice noodles, biscuits or any other foods made from flour, millet, sorghum, maize, rice, wheat or oats
2	11.7	Potatoes, sweet potatoes, beetroots, carrots or any other foods made from these
3	20.2	Other vegetables
4	5.6	Fruits
5	48.5	Beef, pork, lamb, goat, rabbit, wild game, chicken, duck, other birds, chicken heads and feet, liver, kidney, heart, or other organ meats/offal or products
6	5.2	Eggs
7	21.1	Fresh or dried fish or shellfish
8	5.9	Foods made from beans, peas, lentils, or nuts
9	14.2	Cheese, yoghurt, milk or other milk/dairy products
10	29.7	Foods made with oil, fat or butter
11	34.3	Sugar or honey
12	26.7	Other foods such as condiments, coffee, tea

An analysis of the distribution of types of food consumed by food security status shows one major similarity and several important differences in dietary composition (Table 18):

- For every food group (with two exceptions – 1 and 7) the proportion of food secure households is higher than for food insecure households;

- The vast majority of both food secure and food insecure households consume cereals on a daily basis (over 95%);

- Food secure households are more likely to consume meat, dairy products, and potatoes and other tubers. The difference in vegetable consumption is not significant (consumed by 27% of food secure and 21% of food insecure households);

- Although more food secure households consume fruit, the overall proportion is still low (15% versus 4%);

- The only food group from which significantly more food insecure households consumed food was fish (23% versus 13%) which suggests that, for some, fish is a cheaper alternative to meat.

TABLE 18: Type of Foods Consumed by Level of Household Food Security

	Food group	% of food secure households	% of food insecure households
1	Pasta, bread, rice noodles, biscuits or any other foods made from flour, millet, sorghum, maize, rice, wheat or oats	94.9	97.3
2	Potatoes, sweet potatoes, beetroots, carrots or any other foods made from these	25.5	8.9
3	Other vegetables	27.0	20.1
4	Fruits	14.6	4.2
5	Beef, pork, lamb, goat, rabbit, wild game, chicken, duck, other birds, chicken heads and feet, liver, kidney, heart, or other organ meats/offal or products	78.8	45.6
6	Eggs	12.4	4.0
7	Fresh or dried fish or shellfish	13.1	23.3
8	Foods made from beans, peas, lentils or nuts	8.8	5.6
9	Cheese, yoghurt, milk, or other milk/dairy products	26.3	12.8
10	Foods made with oil, fat or butter	54.0	25.5
11	Sugar or honey	55.5	30.8
12	Other foods such as condiments, coffee, tea	49.6	23.4

7.3 Household Expenditure on Food

In order to assess the food purchasing patterns of households in Windhoek, it is necessary to understand how much household income is spent on food. As a whole, the surveyed households spent 21% of their income on food and groceries (with a mean figure of NAD1,033) in the month prior to the survey. The next highest expense category was transportation, followed by telecommunications and then housing (Table 19). The proportion of households spending income on particular items was highest for food and groceries (at 95%), followed by public utilities (60%), transportation (51%), telecommunications (35%), fuel (31%) and housing (26%). Average expenditure on housing, household goods, education, insurance and debt repayments exceeded the average amount spent on food.

TABLE 19: Patterns of Household Expenditure in Windhoek

	% of total expenditures	% of households	Mean monthly expenditures (NAD)
Food and groceries	21.3	95.3	1,033.45
Housing	5.9	26.3	2,667.87
Clothing	3.5	15.7	974.83
Transportation	11.4	51.1	738.49
Telecommunications	7.7	34.6	221.45
Household furniture, tools and appliances	2.5	11.3	1,562.14
Medical care	4.2	18.7	846.61
Education	4.5	19.9	1,141.78
Entertainment	1.5	6.5	878.73
Insurance	2.2	10.0	1,570.28
Debt repayments	1.4	6.1	1,750.26
Donations, gifts	2.8	12.5	968.12
Public utilities (water, electricity, sanitation)	13.4	60.1	864.37
Informal utilities (water, electricity, sanitation)	2.7	12.0	358.99
Fuel	7.3	31.4	200.67
Cash remittances to rural areas	4.1	17.9	1,022.18
Savings	3.4	15.1	3,875.77
Other monthly expenses	0.2	1.0	2,944.56
Total	100.0		6,234.17

As a general rule, the poorer the household, the greater the proportion of total income a household spends. This is confirmed in Windhoek by Table 20, which shows the relationship between household expenditure and income levels in Windhoek. The proportion of household income spent on food and groceries varies from 15% for those in the highest income quintile to 32% for those in the lowest income quintile. As income increases, so the percentage of income spent on food consistently declines. A similar pattern was observed for public utilities and fuel (with low-income households spending a greater proportion of their income than higher income households). The opposite is true for many other categories of expenditure including housing, clothing, transportation, telecommunications, entertainment and insurance.

There is a direct relationship between food expenditure and lived poverty. The poorer the household on the LPI scale, the greater the proportion of income spent on food. Households with an LPI score of less than 1.00 spend about 19% compared to households with an LPI score of 3.00 at more than 30%. The proportion of household income spent on food also varies with other household characteristics (Table 21). For example, food insecure households spend 22% of household income on food and groceries while food secure households spend 18%. Households in informal structures tend to spend more on food than those in formal housing (25% versus 19%). Smaller households spend a greater proportion of their income on food than larger households. Female-centred households spend a greater proportion (24%) than other household types.

TABLE 20: Household Expenditure by Income Quintiles					
	Income quintile				
	I	II	III	IV	V
Food and groceries	32.2	27.0	24.5	20.4	15.0
Housing	2.5	5.4	7.3	7.0	7.3
Clothing	1.9	1.4	2.2	4.4	5.7
Transportation	9.8	9.6	11.4	13.2	12.6
Telecommunications	5.5	6.4	7.7	7.4	9.5
Household furniture, tools and appliances	0.8	1.8	2.7	2.7	3.8
Medical care	3.0	3.4	2.9	3.0	4.6
Education	2.5	4.4	3.6	3.7	5.0
Entertainment	0.0	1.0	0.0	1.2	3.1
Insurance	0.5	0.4	0.5	0.5	3.4
Debt repayments	0.5	0.8	1.5	0.8	1.8
Donations, gifts	1.4	2.0	2.7	1.8	2.7
Public utilities (water, electricity, sanitation)	17.2	18.4	16.2	11.7	11.2
Informal utilities (water, electricity, sanitation)	4.1	3.2	2.9	2.8	1.1
Fuel	15.3	10.6	7.5	6.9	2.3
Cash remittances to rural areas	1.6	2.8	4.4	6.4	5.5
Savings	1.1	1.4	2.2	6.0	5.3
Other monthly expenses	0.5	0.0	0.0	0.3	0.6

TABLE 21: Proportion of Income Spent on Food by Household Characteristics		
Household characteristics		% of income
Food security	Food secure	17.6
	Food insecure	22.3
Housing type	Formal	18.6
	Informal	24.6
Household size	1 member	24.9
	2-3 members	24.0
	4-5 members	19.7
	6 or more members	20.0
Household structure	Female-centred	23.6
	Male-centred	23.4
	Nuclear	20.6
	Extended	18.4
Lived Poverty Index	<=1.00	19.0
	1.01-2.00	26.6
	2.01-3.00	28.9
	3.01-4.00	30.3

8. SUPERMARKET PATRONAGE IN WINDHOEK

8.1 Main Sources of Food

Households in Windhoek obtain food predominantly by purchasing it. Less than 15% of surveyed households obtain food directly from rural areas, less than 5% are involved in urban agriculture and fewer than 3% access food through formal and informal social protection channels (such as sharing, borrowing, community kitchens, food banks etc.). The vast majority of surveyed households rely on food purchase from three main sources: supermarkets, open markets and street vendors. Other food purchase sources include spazas/tuck shops, small shops and fast food/take away outlets. Figure 24 clearly shows the market dominance of supermarkets. Over 90% of surveyed households across the city purchase food at supermarkets, far higher than any other food source. Food insecure households are almost as likely as food secure households to patronize supermarkets (96% versus 99%). Food insecure households are more likely to obtain food from open markets (54% versus 28%) and street vendors (31% versus 20%). Food secure households are marginally more likely to patronize spazas/tuck shops (22% versus 18%) and significantly more likely to consume fast food (28% versus 5%) and patronize restaurants (18% versus 3%).

The dominance of supermarkets is replicated irrespective of whether a household is in formal or informal housing. Over 90% of households in both types purchase food from supermarkets (Figure 25). Households in informal areas are more likely to patronize open markets but, contrary to expectations, less likely to buy food from spazas/tuck shops and street vendors than those in formal housing.

FIGURE 24: Food Sources by Level of Household Food Security

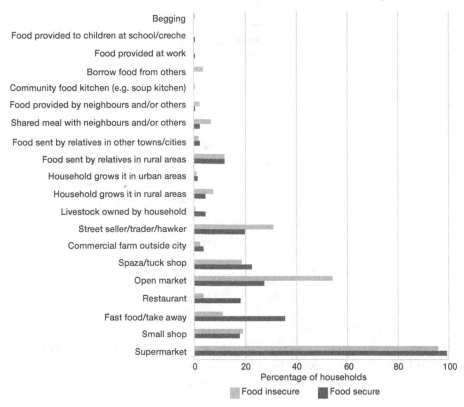

FIGURE 25: Food Sources by Type of Housing

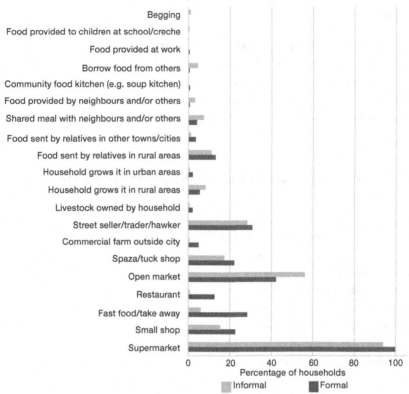

8.2 Frequency of Food Purchase

This section takes the analysis of food sourcing patterns a step further to examine how frequently households purchase food and whether there are differences in the frequency of patronage of different types of retail outlet. In general, 16% of surveyed households purchase food on a daily basis (at least five days per week), 30% do so at least once per week and 38% at least once per month. Figure 26 shows that purchasing behaviour differs between households in formal and informal housing areas. In general, households in more formal housing tend to buy food more frequently than those in informal areas. On the other hand, households in informal housing are more likely to purchase food on a monthly basis.

The next question is whether households purchase food more often at some outlets than others and, in particular, how often they go to the supermarket (Table 22). Of the 97% of households that shop at supermarkets, two-thirds do so monthly. Another 17% shop at supermarkets on a weekly basis and only 5% are daily shoppers. The patronage pattern is very different for both spazas/tuck shops and street vendors. Around half of those who purchase food from these outlets do so on a daily basis, another

35-40% purchase weekly and only 7% do so monthly. The patronage pattern is different again with open markets and small shops. Households are most likely to purchase food at open markets on a weekly basis (with 18% shopping daily, 20% monthly and 17% even less frequently). Small shops (which includes butcheries and bakeries) are most often patronized on a weekly basis (60%). Although the numbers spending money on fast food and in restaurants are lower, many of those households patronize these outlets on a weekly or monthly basis. The contrast in patronage frequency between largely informal sector and/or small business vendors and the supermarkets is therefore dramatic, which raises important questions about what kinds of products are bought at supermarkets versus other outlets.

FIGURE 26: Frequency of Food Purchase by Type of Housing

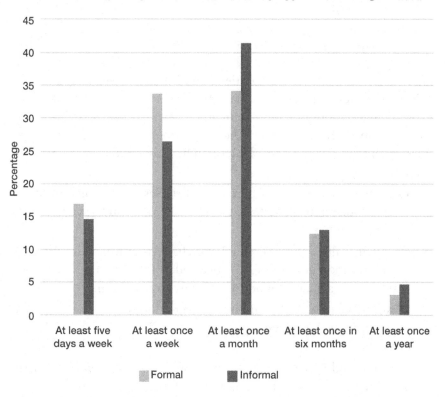

	% of house-holds	Frequency of purchase from the source (%)				
		At least five days per week	At least once per week	At least once per month	At least once in six months	At least once per year
TABLE 22: Frequency of Sourcing Food from Different Outlets						
Supermarket	96.5	4.5	16.5	65.7	12.4	0.8
Small shop	18.6	11.9	60.0	22.5	5.6	0.0
Fast food/ take away	15.5	5.1	39.4	48.5	4.8	2.3
Restaurant	5.8	8.2	49.0	36.7	4.1	2.0
Open market	49.8	17.6	46.2	19.5	16.2	0.5
Spaza/tuck shop	19.4	50.9	41.2	7.3	0.6	0.0
Street seller/ trader/hawker	29.2	49.8	33.7	6.8	9.6	0.0

8.3 Supermarket Domination of Food Purchasing

The survey used the Hungry Cities Food Purchases Matrix (HCFPM) (Crush and McCordic 2017), which captures how many households purchase a range of common food items and where they get them from. The first column in Table 23 shows the proportion of households that purchase each food item on a regular basis. The most striking findings are as follows:

- Over 50% of households purchase all staples, with maize meal the most popular (76%), followed by bread (57%) and rice and pasta (around 50%);

- Less than half of the households purchase fresh products, although meat is the most popular (42%), followed by fish (33%) and vegetables (31%). Only a quarter of households buy fruit and milk;

- Fresh chicken meat is bought by only 9% of households, while frozen (imported) chicken is more popular at 29%. Frozen meat and fish are not popular;

- Cooked food is not purchased by many households, with less than 10% buying a variety of common street foods;

- Processed foods show considerable consumption variation with some, such as cooking oil (76%), sugar (65%) and tea/coffee (46%) very popular. Canned foods are purchased by less than 10% of households; and

- The proportion of households buying "junk" foods is not especially high, although a quarter do buy sugary cooldrinks.

As Table 23 clearly demonstrates, supermarkets are the main source of almost all food products. In the case of half of the products on the list, supermarkets command over 90% of the market share. The three main staples – maize meal, rice and pasta – are bought almost exclusively at supermarkets. In sum, supermarkets completely dominate the food retail system of the city, irrespective of the location, wealth and level of poverty and food insecurity of households. The informal food economy is therefore far more marginal in Windhoek than in many other Southern African cities.

The only staple in which supermarkets face competition is bread although they still command over half of the custom. Supermarkets are also the major source of fresh and frozen produce. Over three-quarters of the households that purchase milk, eggs, fruit, fresh chicken and vegetables do so from supermarkets. In the case of fresh fish, there is some competition from street vendors and open markets. Meat is also bought from small shops (mainly butcheries) and open markets and offal from open markets and street vendors. It is possible, however, that some street vendors and vendors in open markets source their products from supermarkets as well. Supermarkets completely dominate the market for frozen produce and processed foodstuffs. Supermarkets command over 50% of the cooked food market, although fast food outlets do compete for cooked chicken and meat. At least one of these outlets, Hungry Lion, is owned by the supermarket chain, Shoprite.

As demonstrated earlier, South African supermarkets have a strong presence in Windhoek. However, they are not the only players in the food system as there are several locally owned competitors, notably Woermann Brock. In this study, over half of the respondents (57%) said that they patronize South African supermarkets, while the remainder (43%) patronize Namibian supermarkets (with 32% patronizing Woermann Brock). Table 24 provides a breakdown of patronage patterns of the South African supermarkets. Shoprite is clearly the dominant South African chain, with two-thirds (68%) of the households patronizing their Shoprite, Checkers and Usave supermarkets. Around 17% shop at Usave (the subsidiary that targets lower-income areas of cities).

The South African supermarkets appear to be more accessible than local supermarkets for households in informal housing: 54% patronize South African outlets compared to only 30% in formal housing. The majority of households (70%) in the formal housing areas shop at local supermarkets (Figure 27). This suggests that although South African supermarkets are targeting higher-income areas of the city, they are attracting more customers in low-income and informal urban areas. Local supermarkets tend to follow the conventional strategy of targeting middle and high-income areas and consumers.

TABLE 23: HCFPM of Food Item Sources

	% of house-holds buying item	Super-market	Fast food	Small shop	Open market	Spaza/tuck shop	Street vendor
Staples							
Maize meal	75.9	96.0	0.0	1.3	0.6	1.3	0.1
Bread	57.3	53.5	0.0	14.6	1.2	27.8	0.6
Rice	53.2	99.4	0.0	0.2	0.4	0.0	0.0
Pasta	50.6	99.6	0.0	0.0	0.2	0.2	0.0
Fresh produce							
Meat	42.4	61.1	0.0	13.3	20.0	0.3	5.1
Vegetables	31.2	77.5	0.0	1.8	11.6	1.1	8.0
Fish	32.7	46.0	0.0	4.2	16.6	2.4	26.6
Milk	25.4	96.9	0.0	1.3	0.4	0.4	0.9
Eggs	21.4	93.1	0.0	0.0	0.0	3.7	2.1
Fruit	16.7	91.1	0.0	0.6	5.7	0.0	2.5
Offal	11.0	38.1	0.0	9.2	29.9	2.1	18.6
Chicken	8.6	84.5	0.0	1.2	9.5	1.2	2.4
Frozen produce							
Chicken	28.9	95.7	0.0	1.6	0.0	0.4	2.3
Meat	10.1	93.3	0.0	3.4	3.4	0.0	0.0
Fish	7.3	80.0	0.0	0.0	15.4	3.1	1.5
Cooked food							
Pies/vetkoek	9.4	53.0	4.8	3.6	9.6	18.1	10.8
Meat	3.8	51.1	18.2	0.0	27.3	0.0	3.0
Chicken	2.7	62.5	33.3	4.2	0.0	0.0	0.0
Fish	1.0	64.0	4.0	0.0	24.0	4.0	0.0
Processed food							
Cooking oil	75.5	94.6	0.0	2.1	0.7	1.2	0.0
Sugar	64.5	94.7	0.0	0.9	0.5	3.2	0.2
Tea/coffee	46.2	96.8	0.0	1.0	0.5	1.0	0.0
Butter/margarine	26.1	99.6	0.0	0.0	0.0	0.4	0.0
Cooldrinks	23.4	81.2	1.0	3.4	0.5	13.5	0.0
Fruit juice	14.7	97.7	0.0	0.8	0.0	1.5	0.0
Sour milk/omaere	12.3	95.4	0.0	0.0	2.8	1.8	0.0
Snacks (crisps etc)	11.4	66.3	0.0	3.0	2.0	11.9	14.9
Sweets/chocolate	10.5	57.0	0.0	3.2	4.3	18.3	15.1
Canned vegetables	9.7	100.0	0.0	0.0	0.0	0.0	0.0
Canned meat	4.9	95.3	0.0	2.3	2.3	0.0	0.0
Canned fruit	4.7	100.0	0.0	0.0	0.0	0.0	0.0

TABLE 24: Popularity of Different South African Supermarkets

	No.	% of households
Shoprite	316	68.1
Pick n Pay	80	17.2
Checkers	34	7.3
Metro Cash & Carry	15	3.2
Spar	11	2.4
OK Foods	6	1.3
Fruit & Veg City	1	0.2
Game	1	0.2
Total	464	100.0

FIGURE 27: South African and Local Supermarket Patronage by Type of Housing

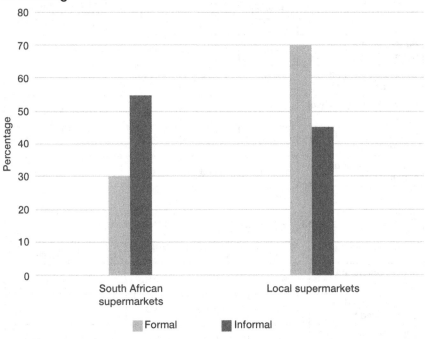

8.4 Consumer Attitudes to Supermarkets

In this section of the report, we examine local attitudes towards super-markets in the city. First, with regard to consumers, the household survey makes it clear that most households in the city obtain some of their food at supermarkets. As part of the survey, respondents who shopped at supermarkets were asked why they did so. Those who did not were asked why they avoided shopping at supermarkets. In both cases, respondents were presented with a series of statements and asked to rank them on a five-point scale from strongly agree to strongly disagree. Of the over 800 respondents who shop at supermarkets, 88% agreed/strongly agreed that one of the primary reasons was the variety of foods in supermarkets (Table 25). Other factors with which there was strong agreement was the sales and discounts offered by supermarkets (82%), the better quality of food (81%) and the opportunities to buy in bulk (76%). Supermarket prices were not nearly as strong an incentive. Less than half (44%) agreed that food was cheaper at supermarkets and as many as 50% disagreed with the statement. Of the smaller number of respondents who never shopped at supermarkets, 78% agreed/strongly agreed that the reason was that supermarkets did not offer credit. Other important disincentives were that supermarkets are too expensive (71%), are only for the wealthy (61%) and are too far away (52%) (Table 26).

TABLE 25: Reasons for Shopping at Supermarkets

	Strongly agree	Some-what agree	Neither	Some-what disagree	Strongly disagree
Supermarkets have a greater variety of foods	65.1	23.0	2.7	6.2	3.0
Supermarkets offer sales and discounts	60.6	21.7	3.9	6.4	7.4
Food is better quality at supermarkets	58.0	23.1	5.5	5.5	8.0
We can buy in bulk at supermarkets	50.5	25.9	3.3	8.0	12.3
Food is cheaper at supermarkets	30.1	14.3	6.0	12.3	37.2

TABLE 26: Reasons for Not Shopping at Supermarkets

	Strongly agree	Somewhat agree	Neither	Somewhat disagree	Strongly disagree
Supermarkets are too expensive	67.7	3.2	12.9	12.9	3.2
Supermarkets do not provide credit	66.7	10	3.3	13.3	6.7
Supermarkets are too far away	48.4	3.2	3.2	16.1	29.0
Supermarkets are only for the wealthy	38.7	22.6	6.5	29.0	3.2
Supermarkets do not sell the food we need	16.7	13.3	10.0	13.3	46.7

The qualitative interviews probed for these and other reasons for the popularity of supermarkets. One of the key motivating factors for patronage appeared to be supermarket sales. Some described a pattern of shopping at multiple supermarkets to take advantage of sales, and shopping only once or twice a month by buying staples in bulk:

I buy mainly in Shoprite, Pick n Pay, Checkers and sometimes in Spar because I check where there is a sale. The type of food I buy is mainly macaroni, rice, cooking oil and meat which I can buy maybe twice a month (Interview No. 1, Moses Garoeb).

If I want to do a proper grocery, including detergent, then at least I will use NAD2,000. I mostly buy in Metro, OK Foods at Baines and Spar. I buy staple food like rice, maize meal, meat, vegetables, coffee and tea. I try to do big shopping once a month and I only add products every week or every second week. I have noticed people tend to use shops that are close to their work places (Interview No. 2, Windhoek West).

I use about NAD900 to buy food per month and I only buy food except relish and meat. I buy maize meal, cooking oil, macaroni, beans, mayonnaise and whatever we need and this can last up to 23rd of that month and then I have to supplement. I buy in Shoprite, Namica and Cash & Carry and sometimes at Woermann Brock because there it's better (Interview No. 3, Tobias Hainyeko).

One respondent was more cynical about supermarket sales and the supposed manipulation of food prices:

Sale price is good because it reduces the budget slightly except at Woermann Brock. But these supermarkets are very smart, if they reduce the price of cooking oil then they increase the price of sugar but you need both of them, so in the end you do not benefit from the sale, it is just the same price (Interview No. 5, John Pandeni).

As noted above, supermarket shopping tends to be a monthly activity for many people, primarily because they buy staples – such as maize meal, rice and macaroni – in bulk quantities. It is noticeable that the supermarkets have responded to this buying pattern, particularly in lower-income communities, by stocking large bags or sacks of these products for purchase.

An earlier study by one of the authors examined the food purchasing patterns of women living in informal settlements in Windhoek and provides insights into why supermarket patronage is lower in low-income communities (Nickanor 2014). These informants made a number of relevant observations about their interactions with supermarkets. One of the major constraints is lack of refrigeration so that fresh produce, when it can be afforded, has to be purchased extremely frequently:

I don't go hungry but I don't eat the kind of food I want to because I cannot afford it. When my boyfriend gives me money I usually go buy food in Shoprite, Stop n Shop, but potatoes I usually buy from the bus stop because a bag costs too much (at Shoprite) (Interview No 14).

We buy fish from local guys who are selling from door to door and one fish costs about NAD3. This is unlike Shoprite or Checkers where fish is neatly packed in a box although it is expensive. We often do not buy fish in large quantities, after all one has nowhere to store it. Shops like Shoprite offer regular discounts as compared to the local shops so you can compare prices before you buy. At times even if you buy where there are discounts, you have to transport goods and this is costly so at the end you have not saved anything. So it's best we buy from local shops here (Interview No. 19).

We purchase food here at the shops. I buy at Shoprite and Woermann Brock. Those are the only places you can buy food at a slightly better quantity, but meat we buy at the bus stops because it's much better than in the formal shops (Interview No. 32).

When we get money then we buy maize flour which lasts five days, but meat or fish you have to buy every day because we do not have electricity in order for us to buy a fridge where we can store our meat and perishables. Thus for every meal you buy a piece of meat or fish which is just enough for that time (Interview No. 23).

Every decent meal consists usually of maize meal or mahangu pap eaten with dried fish or meat when there is money to purchase the meat or fish. That is what we eat here every day. Even if you find chicken or vegetables on sale in the formal shops you will not buy it. Where are you going to store it? There is no electricity here and no refrigerator (Interview No. 26).

Others referred to the constraint of distance from supermarket outlets, which forces them to buy more expensive products in the neighbourhood:

When there is no money then it's a struggle. At times I use NAD1,000 per month buying food only. This informal settlement (Havanna) is far from the main town and any other retail shops. Furthermore, there is no tarred road here and taxis hardly want to bring people this side if they do not charge exorbitant amounts. We are really far from town – the closest food store is the Woermann Brock in Wanaheda, but you can't foot there. There are local shops here but they are much more expensive (Interview No. 27).

I use a lot of money to buy food and we buy it from formal retail shops at Shop n Stop. There is also a local shop here where we buy from because if you compare the prices it does not matter. At the end of the day you end up paying more for transport. (Interview No. 41).

Shoprite, Woermann Brock and Pick n Pay are our preferred shops, but they are far from us. Maybe if they set up their shops here we will get electricity. For now we use a lot of money on transport to go to those shops, especially when you hear that there is a sale. A 50kg bag of maize is cheaper in those shops as compared to our local shops here. But you have to pay the taxi driver double to bring you up to your house with your goods (Focus Group No. 2).

8.5 Labour Disputes With Supermarkets

Very little information is available on the employment practices, working conditions and levels of employee satisfaction at South African supermarkets in Namibia. Recently, however, a series of labour-related incidents took place at Namibian Shoprite stores, leading to a national campaign urging consumers to boycott all Shoprite-owned retailers. The Namibian Commercial Catering, Food and Allied Workers' Union (NACCAFWU) together with Shoprite workers pledged to pressure Shoprite to increase its workers' wages (Kapitako 2017a). This national campaign follows several years of labour disputes between Shoprite and the group's Namibian employees. A labour strike legal process has also been formalized with the labour commissioner issuing a certificate of unresolved dispute in February 2017 (Kapitako 2017b). Over 100 workers have been charged and face dismissal after participating in illegal strikes (Katjanga 2017).

The Namibian Minister of Labour, Erkki Nghimtina, strongly criticized Shoprite, saying that the group was exploitative and was undermining the job security of over 4,300 workers in the country. Nghimtina told media in Windhoek of his great concern that "the unhappy state of labour relations and instability continues at Shoprite, and that the low wages and poor conditions of employment persist and Shoprite remains anti-union. This does not reflect sound labour relations." He urged Shoprite to "turn over a new page in labour relations in Namibia by reaching a mutually acceptable settlement with the workers, and for the company to fully practise our local labour laws, rather than importing their own" (Katjangu 2017). Poor wages and benefits are high among the objections, which include the company's practice of hiring employees on a "permanent part-time" basis where they have no job security and are paid NAD240 per week. Almost 80% of the Shoprite workforce in Namibia is employed on this basis (Kapitako 2017b). These employees do not have fixed schedules, are paid less per hour than full-time employees, work an average of 30 hours per week, and some have worked in this permanent part-time status for more than a decade. Shoprite has been accused of violating Namibian labour regulations in not having formal internal grievance procedures or a disciplinary code, as well as of improper treatment of workers by management. Shoprite employees are reportedly among the most poorly paid workers in Namibia's retail sector (Kapitako 2017b).

To be recognized by Shoprite as the representative union, the Namibian Food and Allied Workers' Union (NAFAU) began a drive to sign up all Shoprite employees as members and called on Shoprite's management not to delay the process of recognition once it reached the required majority membership. NAFAU general secretary Jacob Penda said that "it is a pity that these workers have been divided for the past seven years, and as a result, no union is recognised by Shoprite. This has made the workers vulnerable in terms of rights and representation" (Nakashole 2017). If recognized, the union promised to negotiate for better wages and benefits, in line with those of Shoprite employees in South Africa. A public protest organized by the Economic and Social Justice Trust and others to highlight the plight of Shoprite workers was held in Windhoek in June 2017 (New Era 2017). One of the demands was that Shoprite drop disciplinary charges against over 100 of its employees in Windhoek, relating to a strike in 2015.

Two of the parties in the dispute, the Employers' Association (backing Shoprite) and the Namibia Wholesale and Retail Workers' Union (NWRWU), criticized the Minister of Labour for failing to resolve the issue. NWRWU called for the Minister's resignation in August 2017, and demanded that the President revoke Shoprite's trading licence in Namibia. In a clear reference to the South African origins of Shoprite, NWRWU general secretary Victor Hamunyela said in a statement that "it does not make sense that you are made a slave by people who are in the country at your mercy" (New Era 2017).

9. Impact of Supermarkets on Informal Food Sector

Windhoek's informal sector has not attracted much research attention. This may be partly because it is relatively small compared to many other African cities. Frayne (2004) argued that the sector is "poorly developed" and that although it appears to be expanding, it is doing so slowly. The relatively small size of the informal economy was confirmed by the 2008 Namibian Labour Force Survey which found that there were 64,502 informal employees (including unpaid family members) and 16,856 informal employers (including self-employed individuals) in urban Namibia (Budlender 2011: 9), or a total of 80,908 people working in this sector (compared to 121,077 in the urban formal sector). This suggests that 40% of urban employers and employees are in the informal sector and 60% are in the formal sector. However, if we look only at the sectoral breakdown, a different picture emerges. There were only 21,824 informal employers and employees involved in trade in urban areas, which amounts to 11% of total employment and 27% of total informal employment (Budlender 2011: 31). In terms of the gender breakdown in the informal trade sector countrywide, 61% were women. Informal trade (which includes the informal food sector) is thus dominated by women. Budlender (2011: 38) also provides information on where informal traders and their employees are located in urban areas: in total there were 2,079 individuals trading in markets, 1,779 from street stalls and 4,944 mobile vendors.

The other important feature of the informal sector in Namibia, besides its small size, is the high rate of business failure. The 2008 survey found that half of the employers and employees in the country's informal economy had been working there for less than a year and only 10% had been working for more than five years (Budlender 2011: 62). As many as 90% of small and medium enterprises in Namibia are estimated to collapse within the first five years of operation (Amwele 2013: 1, Kambwale et al 2015). In the evocative language of Ogbokor and Ngeendepi (2012), the majority "crash land during the first 24 months of their existence and in most cases before fully taking-off." One of the main reasons is that "SMEs are easily crowded out of business due to the stiff competition that they get from the already established large scale businesses that currently operate in Namibia" (Ogbokor and Ngeendepi 2012). Or again, "Namibian SMEs have to contend with well-established competitors from South Africa, whose capacity and past experience enable their business practices to see off competition from small Namibian business" (Amwele 2013: 7). The sample size of Amwele's (2013) investigation of the challenges faced by food sector SMEs in Windhoek was too small to draw any definitive conclusions although competition (along with financing and the external operating environment) were identified as important obstacles in the study as a whole. The study does conclude that SMEs in the food and beverage sector face "fierce" competition from Pick n Pay, Woermann Brock, Shoprite and Usave (Amwele 2013: 52).

A third distinctive feature of the informal food sector in Namibia is that most participants are survivalists who have been pushed into food retail by the lack of alternative income-generating opportunities. This emerges particularly clearly in Nickanor's (2014) analysis of the severe difficulties faced by women operating in the food economy in the informal settlements of Windhoek. While the dominance of the food system by supermarkets cannot be held exclusively responsible for the difficulties in the informal food sector, the supermarkets clearly provide an extremely competitive operating environment, particularly as they edge closer to the low-income areas of the city and stock staple products in bulk. Their competitive prices force informal vendors to have very low mark-ups and use what little profit they make to support the basic needs of the household rather than invest in business expansion.

The interviews with informal food vendors revealed some differences of opinion about whether supermarkets were a competitive boon or a competitive threat. Many complained about the negative impact:

> I do not really feel happy about the ever-growing supermarkets in our area. Like now the new Woermann Brock at Monte Cristo service station took some of our customers. These shops are providing competition for me and my profit has decreased over the past months. Here we are only remaining with those customers that are not able to go buy at these shops or we can only get customers after hours when the shops are closed (Interview No. 8).

> Competition from supermarkets is always there. I can give you an example of stuff that can go without selling if there is a special in supermarkets. My milk I sell at NAD19.50 but will reduce whether there is a sale in town or not. Like in shops now, it is NAD13 so I don't do business like I always do (Interview No. 9).

> People from this area always go shop from supermarkets if they find out that I do not sell the goods that they are looking for. These shops are giving us difficulties in selling our goods sometimes. Most of the time people buy from the supermarkets on their way from work and end up not buying from our stands. I throw away all foods that I am not able to sell when they are spoiled. Sometimes I reduce the prices of the foods that I am not able to sell over a long period to avoid making a loss for that particular month (Interview No. 11).

> It is not a good thing at all, because us that are selling in streets near these shops are losing customers. Yes, they are giving me competition. The supermarkets have affected my business in a way that if my prices are high, then people just go buy in supermarkets instead (Interview No. 17).

> It is a bad thing. Most of our customers are now going to these shops instead of buying from the stalls here. Now we are no longer getting customers in the open market like in the past (Interview No. 18).

Those with a narrow market niche and customer base, as well as greater distance from supermarkets, did not see the distribution and activities of supermarkets as a threat:

> The increase in supermarkets does not affect my business because there are a lot of people. Like, for example, these 20 loaves of bread will finish when people are knocking off work, as they are passing by to their homes (Interview No. 3).

These supermarkets do not give me a competition, since they are operating from far. My business is not directly affected, because I am just targeting school children and households in this street and nearby streets (Interview No. 4).

Supermarkets are not giving me competition at all, since I am only selling cooked (food) and those that are not able to buy in supermarkets buy their lunch from me. Like here, I am selling in front of Wernhill Park, there are many shops there that are selling food and people still prefer to buy here (Interview No. 16).

It is actually a good thing that there are more supermarkets now. People now have the power to decide where they want to buy from and they also have many shops to choose from now in terms of price preferences. The supermarkets are not giving me any competition at all, even their own employees come buy from me. If there was a competition, I would not be having supermarket employees as my customers (Interview No. 13).

The results from the household food purchases matrix analysis clearly show that the informal food sector is only able to compete with supermarkets on a few products (Table 27). For example, open markets are a source of meat, offal, vegetables and fish (fresh and frozen) as well as cooked meat and fish. Spazas/tuck shops are patronized for bread, pies/*vetkoek* and snacks and street vendors have a share of the market for fresh fish and offal. However, in almost every case, supermarkets have a greater market share than informal vendors. There is only one product – offal – where the informal sector has a greater market share than the supermarkets, although supermarkets close to low-income areas of the city are increasing their stock of offal and already command nearly 40% of the market.

TABLE 27: HCFPM of Selected Food Item Sources

	Supermarket	Open market	Spaza/ tuck shop	Street vendor
Bread	53.5	1.2	27.8	0.6
Meat	61.1	20.0	0.3	5.1
Vegetables	77.5	11.6	1.1	8.0
Fish	46.0	16.6	2.4	26.6
Offal	38.1	29.9	2.1	18.6
Frozen fish	80.0	15.4	3.1	1.5
Pies/vetkoek	53.0	9.6	18.1	10.8
Cooked meat	51.1	27.3	0.0	3.0
Cooked fish	64.0	24.0	4.0	0.0
Snacks (crisps etc)	66.3	2.0	11.9	14.9
Sweets/chocolate	57.0	4.3	18.3	15.1

One of the striking features of the informal food vendors in Windhoek is their price sensitivity. Mark-ups are small and they are constantly on the look-out for products with resale potential. This means that they tend to shop from a variety of different outlets. Wholesalers are popular sources of products, as are companies such as MeatCo for meat products. Others source products at supermarkets (particularly when there are sales) but do not tend to patronize only one outlet, purchasing instead at a variety of supermarkets:

> I source my products from Pick n Pay in Katutura, Spar in Khomasdal, fish from Mama Fresh, millet from my mother in the north (50kg every two and a half months). Free range chicken is from Single Quarters. Pick n Pay normally has fresh and clean products unlike Woermann Brock and Shoprite. You can also find most products in Pick n Pay (Interview No. 5).

> Boerewors and meat I buy from Rand St Butchery in Khomasdal. I buy cool drinks from Metro or anywhere there is a sale. Coffee and tea from Pick n Pay, Spar or Metro depending on the price. These shops are cheaper and they are always having food items on sale (Interview No. 12).

> It is cheaper to buy in bulk than buying single items. I buy my potatoes from a vendor in Okuryangava area opposite the clinic. They are cheaper there and big compared to supermarkets. I buy my Russians (sausages) from a shop in Southern Industrial area. Russians are cheaper there. I buy Oros and sweets from Metro. It is close by and they are cheaper compared to buying from Food Lover's Market or Checkers (Interview No. 13).

> I buy meat and cabbage from vendors in Monte Cristo road or in the open market. It is cheaper to buy from them than supermarkets. I buy macaronic, nik-naks, and sugar for Oshikundu and Otombo from Namica supermarket. I send my children to buy there while I am still here selling. The shop is also cheap. I buy Meme mahangu from Shoprite Usave and sorghum from the open market in Okuryangava. Usave and the open market are also at Stop n Shop area where I buy most of my goods. I buy macaroni, Meme mahangu, sugar, baking flour, yeast, soup, cooking oil. These goods are only found in supermarkets (Interview No. 15).

> I only buy top score, 50kg per month. When it is not enough, I add about 25kg in the middle of the month. I also buy tinned fish and this I usually buy from Shoprite and Woermann. I do not buy fruit and vegetables because it is usually just seen as for people who have money. I go to the shop as frequently as I have the money to buy the top score and the tinned fish. The longest I take is two weeks to go

back there. But for meats I have to do it a lot because we do not have means of refrigerating it (Interview No. 8, Okahandja Park Market).

Comparison shopping and multi-sourcing is one strategy successful informal vendors use to survive in this tough competitive environment. Some are also able to acquire and sell traditional products and wild foods not available in supermarkets:

> The products I sell are traditional dry food (which varies depending on the season), *mahangu* flour, beans, chilli, salt, sorghum flour, omutete, ombidi, spices, mopane worms, dry fish, moringa, capenta. You need to have stock and it's not easy to source traditional food; it's not as if you can find them in a market…Around September, chilli will be out of season, dry beans and dry spinach also. In November, we run out of mopane worms so we source them from Angola and Zambia. We have, for example, people who are selling mopane worms in a 50kg bag. If you have a lot of money you can buy the whole 50kg bag or half or whatever. I normally source products from the north, meaning you have to ask people in different homes if they sell (Interview No. 2).

Another reason for business survival is the current geography of the food system. Residents of the informal settlements and the very poor, in particular, still find that physical access to food sources is difficult. While supermarkets are increasingly closing in on these areas, spazas and mobile vendors are still able to market products in their immediate neighbourhoods. In contrast to the general picture of supermarket dominance shown earlier, the pattern of food sourcing among poor households is very different with only 20% patronizing supermarkets. The informal food economy is much more important for these households with street vendors the most important food retail source, followed by open markets, small shops and spaza/tuck shops. On the other hand, these customers, by definition, have very little disposable income and profit margins are slight. As one of Nickanor's (2014) respondents noted: "All I'm doing now is selling *okapana*. What I'm getting from selling is very little and is not much different from those who are not doing anything. But you cannot sit back and do nothing."

In an attempt to improve the operating environment for informal vendors, as well as discourage vendors from selling on the streets, the municipality has constructed a series of open markets where vendors pay a fee in exchange for a stall and access to potable water and ablution facilities. Those who sell in the markets are unhappy with the fees they have to pay to the municipality and complain about unfair competition from street vendors who set up outside the open markets, use the facilities and pay no fees. The spatial distribution of open markets shows that they are targeted at lower-income areas of the city (Figure 29). If the conventional wisdom that supermarkets target only higher-income areas of the African city were correct, these open markets (modelled on formal and informal markets elsewhere) would probably mean greater success for informal vendors. However, as Figure 30 shows, most open markets are clustered in areas of the city where there is a growing supermarket presence.

FIGURE 28: Patronage of Food Sources by Extremely Poor Households

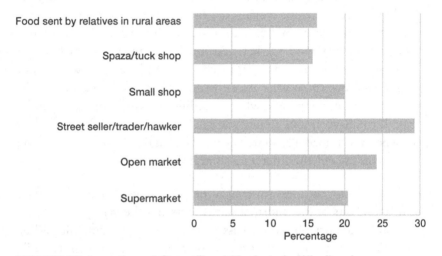

FIGURE 29: Location of Open Food Markets in Windhoek

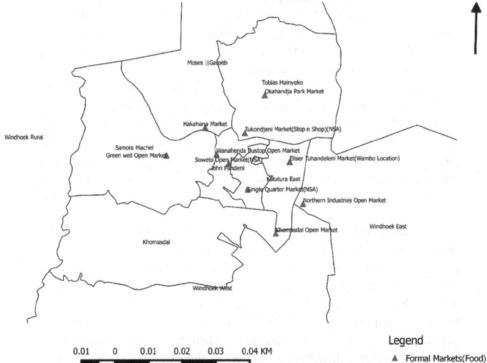

FIGURE 30: Location of Food Outlets in Windhoek

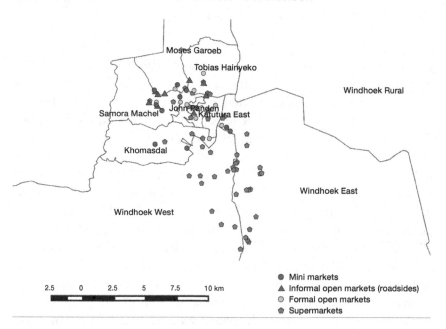

10. CONCLUSION

After 2000, several scholars argued that Africa was undergoing a super-market revolution similar to that which had earlier come to dominate food systems and consumer habits in the Global North and Latin America. They argued that South Africa was the one African country emulating this model and suggested not only that the "supermarket revolution" would spread throughout the continent but that South African-based supermarkets would lead the revolution. The primary reason was that the end of apartheid was opening up the continent to South African business-es, which were attracted by the massive urban consumer market accompanying rapid urbanization and the growth of an African middle-class. The revolution would supposedly benefit consumers and small farmers who would be incorporated into new supermarket food supply chains. The proponents of the supermarket revolution model were primarily agricultural economists who viewed it as a largely inevitable and positive development. However, enthusiasm for the model has waned with much less being written about in the last decade. Political economy analysis has been extremely critical of the modernization premises of the model (the idea of inevitable stages or waves in particular) and the fact that the primary beneficiaries are not consumers or smallholders but large, monopolistic

South African corporations whose bottom lines are flourishing through corporate expansion into the rest of Africa.

Like many cities in Southern Africa, Windhoek has been growing rapidly, primarily as a result of in-migration, especially from the more heavily populated rural north of Namibia. Urban planning has been unable to keep pace with the influx, leading to the expansion of informal settlements to the north of the city. The population of Windhoek has grown from 147,000 at independence in 1990 to 326,000 in 2011 to its current estimated population of 430,000. In 2008, AFSUN conducted a household food security baseline survey in lower-income neighbourhoods of the city (Tobias Hainyeko, Moses Garoeb, Samora Machel and Khomasdal North) (Pendleton et al., 2012). The survey covered around 180,000 people in these four areas, or more than half of the city, and found that 77% of households were food insecure and 23% were food secure. In the informal settlements, 89% were food insecure and 11% were food secure. Dietary diversity was also low at 5.95 (on the HDDS scale) for the sample as a whole and 4.78 for households in informal settlements. The survey also revealed a very high level of supermarket patronage in these lower-income areas of the city, with 83% of households obtaining at least some of their food through supermarket purchase, more than through the informal food sector (at 66%). Urban agriculture was negligible, with less than 5% of households growing any of their own food within the city. Much more important were informal food transfers from rural areas, received by 72% of households.

The surprisingly high rate of supermarket patronage in low-income areas of the city was at odds with conventional wisdom at the time that supermarkets in African cities are primarily patronized by middle and high-income residents and therefore target their neighbourhoods. However, Windhoek was not alone in this respect. Rates of supermarket patronage by low-income urban residents were similarly high in the three South African cities surveyed (Cape Town, Johannesburg and Msunduzi) and in other countries neighbouring South Africa, including Botswana, Lesotho and Swaziland. In other Southern African countries, such as Zimbabwe, Zambia, Malawi and Mozambique, rates of patronage were lower and, simultaneously, informal food sector purchasing was much higher. This raised the obvious question of what was happening in Namibia and other countries that made supermarkets so much more accessible to the urban poor, as well as other questions about what they were buying at supermarkets and how frequently they shopped there. Further, what was the relationship, if any, between supermarkets and informal food vendors? Was there some kind of symbiotic relationship (as there appears to be in many

Asian cities, for example) or were supermarkets driving the informal sector out of business? In South Africa, the government's Competition Commission began investigating this, following numerous complaints about supermarket incursion by owners of small informal food businesses.

What the 2007-2008 AFSUN survey suggested was that the supermarket revolution model was a potentially accurate depiction of countries in the immediate vicinity of South Africa. There were several reasons for this: first, those countries within the Southern African Customs Union and Rand Monetary Area facilitated the ability of South African corporations to do business, move goods across borders and repatriate profits. Second, these countries had a long history of South African corporate investment. Nascent South African supermarket chains had been operating in these countries since at least the 1960s. In the case of Namibia, South Africa's occupation and control of Namibia until 1990 made it easy for South African companies to view the country as a province of South Africa. Third, geographical proximity meant that it was unnecessary for supermarkets to build local supply chains from scratch. Instead, these countries and their cities were simply incorporated into existing supply chains, becoming retail nodes for large-scale South African agricultural producers and food processors. While the AFSUN research was extremely suggestive about the importance of supermarkets to urban food systems in Southern Africa, it was viewed through the narrow lens of the household consumer. The current project was therefore established to investigate the supermarket revolution model in greater depth, beginning with Namibia and then extending to other countries in the region. In addition to exploring questions about supermarket expansion and operations, the project aimed to investigate the implications of South African supermarket growth in other countries including impacts on smallholder farmers, on the informal food system, and on the food environment and food security of households in cities.

Five main conclusions emerge from the research project and findings discussed in this report:

- Namibia in general, and Windhoek in particular, has undergone a partial supermarket revolution focused predominantly at the retail level of the food supply chain. The levels of supermarket concentration in Windhoek are very similar to those in similar-sized South African cities. Namibia is distinctive in that it is the site of intense competition between the major South African supermarkets and a locally owned chain, Woermann Brock. In some countries, such as Kenya, local chains have effectively kept South African chains out of the market. In Namibia, Woermann Brock (with a retail history of more than 120 years) has had to compete with the South African retail giants and has managed to survive and expand. The reasons for its success need more research as a potential model for locally owned companies in other African markets.

- The Namibian supermarket revolution is incomplete in the sense that, unlike in South Africa, it has not involved wholesale transformation of the agro-food system. Some large-scale Namibian farms (particularly in the beef and vegetables sector) have been able to take advantage of new demands from supermarkets, but the overall number of local producer-beneficiaries seems small. Government protectionism has prompted some adjustment in supermarket strategies of procurement (particularly for processed cereal products). New initiatives, such as the Growth at Home Strategy and Namibian Retail Charter, may lead to more local sourcing of products but the main beneficiaries are likely to be large commercial farms and food processors rather than small farmers. Even then, as this report shows, the vast majority of products sold in supermarkets in Windhoek are imported from South Africa. Indeed, Windhoek supermarkets appear to be fully integrated into the same supply and distribution chains as South African cities.

- The obvious question for Namibians is who benefits from the overwhelming presence of South African supermarkets? South Africans? Namibians? Both? Because financial information on the operations, profits and capital flows of the supermarkets are closely guarded corporate secrets it is extremely difficult to quantify these economic impacts. However, we can examine the argument, often made by supermarkets, that the consumer benefits by getting more varied, cheaper, fresher and safer foods. This takes us back to the lens of the consumer. The city-wide household survey conducted for this report is extremely instructive, particularly when compared to the 2008 results, taking into account that the latter focused only on low-income residential areas. The proportion of food insecure households has fallen slightly from 77% to 72% (although the two populations are not strictly comparable since this survey includes middle and high-income households in Windhoek East and West). However, food insecurity has increased in the informal settlements from 89% to 92%. Overall dietary diversity has fallen significantly from 5.95 to 4.47 (and from 4.78 to 2.66 in informal settlements). The obvious conclusion is that supermarkets may be making more food available, but they are not making it more accessible, or accessible enough, to improve food security significantly.

- There are various models of the supermarket-informal vendor relationship, ranging from the informal resilience model in East and Central African cities to the symbiotic model in some South African cities to the destructive-impact model in others. Like South Africa, informal food vending is a relatively recent phenomenon in Namibia and most informal vendors lack their own independent supply chains (with the notable exception of wild foods). What emerges from the interviews with vendors in Windhoek is the tough competitive environment in which they struggle to make a living. They do, at present, have greater patronage in informal settlements, and the city has sought to support vendors and boost accessibility through its system of open markets. However, as in South African cities, the supermarkets are moving closer to the low-income mass market with budget subsidiaries such as Usave. And it is not just staples that are bought at supermarkets, as conventional wisdom suggests. The HCFPM shows that more than half of the households that purchase any food item do so at supermarkets. In many cases, the proportion exceeds 80-90%.

- Timmer's (2017) pessimistic view that the supermarket revolution and its impacts are beyond the control of governments inevitably leads to policy paralysis. Battersby (2017) argues that in South Africa the growth and consolidation of supermarkets has involved food system transformation in the absence of food system planning. Government leads and controls the process of mall development but has no explicit food security or food system mandate. Mallification, including in Namibia, therefore represents other urban planning priorities and interests which see the development of malls as an unmitigated public and private win (for the developer, the tenants and the consumer). The obstacles to developing a coherent food security strategy at the city level are many but not insurmountable (Haysom, 2015). A promising first step was Windhoek's engagement with the food system governance of Belo Horizonte in Brazil and the subsequent 2014 Windhoek Declaration on food security by the mayors of Namibian towns and cities (World Future Council, nd). Unfortunately, the World Future Council does not show how the lessons of Belo Horizonte could be applied in Windhoek and instead defaults to advocating urban agriculture – a strategy that has failed in many other African cities – as the solution to urban food insecurity (Crush et al, 2011). Advocacy and declarations will also make little progress unless they understand the centrality of the supermarket revolution and seek to regulate it in the interests of the urban poor and food insecure. Here, initiatives such as the South African Competition Commission's (2017) Retail Market Enquiry could have potentially important implications for supermarket behaviour and the informal food economy in South African cities. Almost certainly, its findings will have relevance for Namibia which might consider launching its own investigation of the impact of a supermarket revolution that is largely orchestrated from corporate headquarters in South African cities. More generally, we hope that this report will add to the knowledge base for Namibia's mayors as they, and national government, seek to fulfil the promise of the Windhoek Declaration to "engage in a multi-stakeholder dialogue on food and nutrition security governance and interventions at different levels."

REFERENCES

1.   Abrahams, C. (2009). "Transforming the Region: Supermarkets and the Local Food Economy" *African Affairs* 109: 115-134.

2.   Abrahams, C. (2011). "Supermarkets and Urban Value Chains: Rethinking the Developmental Mandate" *Food Chain* 1: 206-222.

3.   Amwele, H. (2013). "An Empirical Investigation into the Factors Affecting the Performance of SMEs in the Retail Sector in Windhoek, Namibia" MIB Thesis, Polytechnic of Namibia, Windhoek.

4.   Andersson, C., Chege, C., Rao, E and Qaim, M. (2015). "Following Up on Smallholder Farmers and Supermarkets in Kenya" *American Journal of Agricultural Economics* 97: 1247–1266.

5.   Andjamba, H. (2017). "Econometric Estimation of the Demand for Meat in Namibia" Magister Scientiae Agriculturae Thesis, University of the Free State, Bloemfontein.

6.   Asfaw, A. (2008). "Does Supermarket Purchase Affect the Dietary Practices of Households? Some Empirical Evidence from Guatemala" *Development Policy Review* 26: 227–243.

7.   Battersby, J. (2017). "Food System Transformation in the Absence of Food System Planning: The Case of Supermarket and Shopping Mall Retail Expansion in Cape Town, South Africa" *Built Environment* 43: 417-430.

8.   Battersby, J. and Peyton, S. (2014). "The Geography of Supermarkets in Cape Town: Supermarket Expansion and Food Access" *Urban Forum* 25: 153-164.

9.   Battersby, J., Marshak, M. and Mngqibisa, N. (2017). *Mapping the Invisible: The Informal Food Economy of Cape Town, South Africa.* AFSUN Report No. 24, Cape Town.

10. Berkowitz, B., Ramkolowan, Y., Stern, M., Venter, F. and Webb, M. (2012). *The Role of South African Business in Africa: South African Outward Investment*. Report for Nedlac, Pretoria.

11. Biénabe, E., Berdegué, J., Peppelenbos, L. and Belt, J. (eds.) (2011). *Reconnecting Markets Innovative Global Practices in Connecting Small-Scale Producers with Dynamic Food Markets* (Farnham: Gower).

12. Blandon, J., Henson, S. and Cranfield, J. (2009). "Small-Scale Farmer Participation in New Agri-Food Supply Chains: Case of the Supermarket Supply Chain for Fruit and Vegetables in Honduras" *Journal of International Development* 21: 971-984.

13. Brown, A. (2015). "Sustaining African Cities: Urban Hunger and Sustainable Development in East Africa" *International Journal of Environmental, Cultural, Economic & Social Sustainability* 11: 1-12.

14. Budlender, D. (2011). *Informal Employment in Namibia in 2008* (Geneva: ILO).

15. Cheadle, H. (2017). "Grocery Retail Market Enquiry Public Hearings: Remarks by the Chairperson" At: http://www.compcom.co.za/wp-content/uploads/2015/06/Cape-Town-Public-Hearings-introduction-by-Prof-Halton-Cheadle.pdf

16. Chidozie, F., Olanrewaju, I. and Akande, O. (2014). "Foreign Megastores and the Nigerian Economy: A Study of Shoprite" *Mediterranean Journal of Social Sciences* 5: 425-437.

17. Ciuri, S. (2013). "Nakumatt Set to Take Over Shoprite Stores in Tanzania" *Business Daily Africa* 17 December.

18. Ciuri, S. and Kisembo, D. (2015). "Uganda: Nakumatt to Buy Shoprite" *All Africa* 23 July.

19. Competition Commission of South Africa (2016). "Enforcement of Competition Policy in the Retail Sector: Contribution by South Africa" Prepared for 2016 UNCTAD Round Table, Geneva.

20. Competition Commission of South Africa (2017). Retail Market Enquiry. At http://www.compcom.co.za/retail-market-inquiry/

21. Coates, J. (2013). "Build it Back Better: Deconstructing Food Security for Improved Measurement and Action" *Global Food Security* 2: 188-194.

22. Crush, J. and Caesar, M. (2016). "Food Access and Insecurity in a Supermarket City" In J. Crush and J. Battersby (eds.), *Rapid Urbanisation, Urban Food Deserts and Food Security in Africa* (New York: Springer), pp. 47-58.

23. Crush, J. and Frayne, B. (2011a). "Urban Food Insecurity and the New International Food Security Agenda" *Development Southern Africa* 28: 527-544.

24. Crush, J. and Frayne, B. (2011b). "Supermarket Expansion and the Informal Food Economy in Southern African Cities: Implications for Urban Food Security" *Journal of Southern African Studies* 37: 781-807.

25. Crush, J., Frayne, B., McLachlan, M. (2011). *Rapid Urbanization and the Nutrition Transition in Southern Africa.* AFSUN Report No. 7, Cape Town.

26. Crush, J., Frayne, B. and Pendleton, W. (2012). "The Crisis of Food Insecurity in African Cities" *Journal of Hunger and Environmental Nutrition* 7: 271-292.

27. Crush, J., Hovorka. A. and Tevera, D. (2011). "Food Security in Southern African Cities: The Place of Urban Agriculture" *Progress in Development Studies* 11: 285-305.

28. Crush, J. and McCordic, C. (2017). "The Hungry Cities Food Purchases Matrix: Household Food Sourcing and Food System Interaction" *Urban Forum* 28: 421-433.

29. Crush, J. and Riley, L. (2017). "Urban Food Security and Rural Bias" HCP Discussion Paper No. 11, Waterloo and Cape Town.

30. Dakora, E. (2012). "Exploring the Fourth Wave of Supermarket Evolution: Concepts of Value and Complexity in Africa" *International Journal of Managing Value and Supply Chains* 3: 25-37.

31. Dakora, E. (2016). "Expansion of South African Retailers' Activities into Africa" Cape Peninsula University of Technology, Cape Town.

32. Dakora, E. and Bytheway, A. (2014). "Entry Mode Issues in the Internationalisation of South African Retailing" *Mediterranean Journal of Social Sciences* 5: 194-205.

33. Dakora, E., Bytheway, A. and Slabbert, A. (2010). "The Africanisation of South African Retailing: A Review" *African Journal of Business Management* 4: 748-754.

34. das Nair, R. (nd). "The Internationalisation of Supermarkets and the Nature of Competitive Rivalry in Retailing in Southern Africa" Centre for Competition, Regulation and Economic Development, University of Johannesburg.

35. das Nair, R. (2015). "The Implications of the Growth of Supermarket Chains in Southern Africa on Competitive Rivalry" Competition Commission and Competition Tribunal's 9th Annual Conference on Competition Law, Economics and Policy, Johannesburg.

36. das Nair, R. and Chisoro, S. (2016). "The Expansion of Regional Supermarket Chains and Implications for Local Suppliers: Capabilities in South Africa, Botswana, Zambia and Zimbabwe" UNU WIDER Working Paper 2016/114, Helsinki.

37. das Nair, R. and Chisoro, S. (2017). "The Expansion of Regional Supermarket Chains: Implications on Suppliers in Botswana and South Africa" UNU WIDER Working Paper 2017/26, Helsinki.

38. das Nair, R. and Dube, C. (2015). "Competition, Barriers to Entry and Inclusive Growth: Case Study on Fruit and Veg City" Working Paper 9/2015, Centre for Competition, Regulation and Economic Development (CCRED), University of Johannesburg.

39. das Nair, R. and Dube, S. (2017). "Growth and Strategies of Large, Lead Firms – Supermarkets" Working Paper 8/2017, CCRED, University of Johannesburg.

40. Dawson, N., Martin, A. and Sikor, T. (2016). "Green Revolution in Sub-Saharan Africa: Implications of Imposed Innovation for the Wellbeing of Rural Smallholders" *World Development* 78: 204-218.

41. Deloitte (2015). *African Powers of Retailing: New Horizons for Growth.* Johannesburg.

42. Dralle, T. (2017). "The South African Walmart/Massmart Case: SME-Friendly Domestic Competition Laws in the Light of International Economic Law" In T. Rensmann (ed.), *Small and Medium Enterprises in International Economic Law* (Oxford: OUP), pp. 123-64.

43. Economist (2013). "The Grocers' Great Trek: A Sluggish Home

Market is Pushing South Africa's Big Retail Chains" *The Economist* 19 September.

44. Emongor, R. (2009). "The Impact of South African Supermarkets on Agricultural and Industrial Development in the Southern African Development Community" PhD Thesis, University of Pretoria, Pretoria.

45. Emongor, R. and Kirsten, J. (2009). "The Impact of South African Supermarkets on Agricultural Development in the SADC: A Case Study in Zambia, Namibia, and Botswana" *Agrekon* 48: 6-84.

46. Farina, E., Nunes, R. and Monteiro, G. (2005). "Supermarkets and Their Impacts on the Agrifood System of Brazil: The Competition Among Retailers" *Agribusiness* 21: 133-147.

47. Frayne, B. (2004). "Migration and Urban Survival Strategies in Windhoek, Namibia" *Geoforum* 35: 489-505.

48. Gengenbach, H., Schurman, R., Bassett, T., Munro, W. and Moseley, W. (2017). "Limits of the New Green Revolution for Africa: Reconceptualising Gendered Agricultural Value Chains" *Geographical Journal* DOI: 10.1111/geoj.12233

49. Gorton, M., Sauer, J. and Supatpongkul, P. (2011). "Wet Markets, Supermarkets and the "Big Middle" for Food Retailing in Developing Countries: Evidence from Thailand" *World Development* 39: 1624-1637.

50. Greenberg, S. (2017). "Corporate Power in the Agro-Food System and the Consumer Food Environment in South Africa" *Journal of Peasant Studies* 44: 467-496.

51. Hawkes, C. (2008). "Dietary Implications of Supermarket Development: A Global Perspective" *Development Policy Review* 26: 657-692.

52. Haysom, G. (2015). "Food and the City: Urban Scale Food System Governance" *Urban Forum* 26: 263-281.

53. Huang, C., Tsai, K. and Chen, Y. (2015). "How Do Wet Markets Still Survive in Taiwan?" *British Food Journal* 117: 234-256.

54. Humphrey, J. (2007). "The Supermarket Revolution in Developing Countries: Tidal Wave or Tough Competitive Struggle?" *Journal of Economic Geography* 7: 433-450.

55. Igumbor, E., Sanders, D., Puoane, T., Tsolekile, L., Schwarz, C., Purdy, C., Swart, R., Durão, S. and Hawkes, C. (2012). "'Big Food," the Consumer Food Environment, Health, and the Policy Response in South Africa" *PLoS Medicine* 9(7): e1001253.

56. Ijuma, C., Snyder, J., Tshirley, D. and Reardon, T. (2015). "Stages of Transformation in Food Processing and Marketing: Results of an Initial Inventory of Processed Food Products in Dar es Salaam, Arusha, and Mwanza" Tanzania Policy Research Brief No. 3, Michigan State University, Ann Arbor.

57. Kaira, C. and Haidula, T. (2014). "Checkers and Shoprite Probed Over Mislabelling" *The Namibian* 11 September.

58. Kalundu, K. and Meyer, F. (2017). "The Dynamics of Price Adjustment and Relationships in the Formal and Informal Beef Markets in Namibia" *Agrekon* 56: 53-66.

59. Kambwale, J., Chisoro, C. and Karodia, J. (2015). "Investigation into the Causes of Small and Medium Enterprise Failures in Windhoek, Namibia" *Arabian Journal of Business and Management Review* 4: 80-109.

60. Kapitako, A. (2017a). "Union Mounts National Campaign to Boycott Shoprite" *New Era* 19 September.

61. Kapitako, A. (2017b). "Shoprite Workers to Vote on Strike" *The Namibian* 21 February.

62. Karaan, M. and Kirsten, J. (2008). "A Programme to Mainstream Black Farmers into Supply Chains: An Emphasis on Fresh Produce" Southern Africa Policy Brief 6, Regoverning Markets Project, IIED, London.

63. Katjangu, N. (2017). "Shoprite Exploitive, says Nghimtina" *The Namibian* 21 July.

64. Kazembe, L. and Nickanor, N. (2017). "Spatial Modelling of the Relationship Between Socio-Economic Disadvantage and Child Health in Namibia" *Spatial Demography* 5: 1-24.

65. Kelly, M., Seubsman, S., Banwell, C. and Dixon, J. (2014). " Thailand's Food Retail Transition: Supermarket and Fresh Market Effects on Diet Quality and Health" *British Food Journal* 116: 1180-1193.

66. Kennedy, G., Nantel, G. and Shetty, P. (2004). "Globalization of Food Systems in Developing Countries: A Synthesis of Country Case Studies" FAO Food and Nutrition Paper 83, Rome.

67. Kenny, B. (2014). "Walmart in South Africa: Precarious Labor and Retail Expansion" *International Labor and Working Class History* 86: 173-177.

68. Kimenju, S., Rischke, R., Klasen, S. and Qaim, M. (2015). "Do Supermarkets Contribute to the Obesity Pandemic in Developing Countries?" *Public Health Nutrition* 18: 3224-3233.

69. Louw, A., Chikazunga, D., Jordaan, D. and Biénabe, E. (2007). "Restructuring Food Markets in South Africa: Dynamics Within the Context of the Tomato Subsector" Agrifood Sector Studies, Regoverning Markets Project, University of Pretoria.

70. Meyer, D. and Keyser, E. (2016). "Validation and Testing of the Lived Poverty Index Scale (LPI) in a Poor South African Community" *Social Indicators Research* 129: 147-159.

71. Michelson, H., Reardon, T., Perez, F. (2012). "Small Farmers and Big Retail: Trade-offs of Supplying Supermarkets in Nicaragua" *World Development* 40: 342–354.

72. Miller, D., Saunders, R. and Oloyede, O. (2008). "South African Corporations and Post-Apartheid Expansion in Africa: Creating a New Regional Space" *African Sociological Review* 12: 1-19.

73. Minten, B., Reardon, T. and Sutradhar, R. (2010). "Food Prices and Modern Retail: The Case of Delhi" *World Development* 38: 1775-1787.

74. Monteiro C., Levy, R., Claro, R., de Castro. I and Cannon G. (2011). "Increasing Consumption of Ultra-Processed Foods and Likely Impact on Human Health: Evidence from Brazil" *Public Health Nutrition* 14: 5-13.

75. Monteiro, C., Moubarac, J.-C., Cannon, G., Ng, S. and Popkin, B. (2013). "Ultra-Processed Products are Becoming Dominant in the Global Food System" *Obesity Reviews* 14(S2): 21-28.

76. Moustier, P., Tam, P., Anh, D., Binh, V. and Loc, N. (2010). "The Role of Farmer Organizations in Supplying Supermarkets with Quality Food in Vietnam" *Food Policy* 35: 69-78.

77. Muchopa, C. (2013). "Agricultural Value Chains and Smallholder Producer Relations in the Context of Supermarket Proliferation in Southern Africa" *International Journal of Managing Value and Supply Chains* 4: 33-44.

78. Nakashole, N. (2017). "Nafau wants all Shoprite Workers to Join one Union" *The Namibian* 18 May.

79. New Era (2017). "Union Challenges Nghimtina over Shoprite Workers" *New Era* 17 August.

80. NPC (nd). *Namibia Poverty Mapping* (Windhoek: National Planning Commission).

81. Nickanor, N. (2014). "Food Deserts and Household Food Insecurity in the Informal Settlements of Windhoek, Namibia" PhD Thesis, University of Cape Town, Cape Town.

82. Nortons Inc (2016). "Grocery Retail Sector Market Inquiry: Pick n Pay Submission" Johannesburg.

83. Ogbokor, C. and Ngeendepi, E. (2012). "Investigating the Challenges Faced by SMEs in Namibia" Department of Economics, Polytechnic of Namibia, Windhoek.

84. Olbrich, R., Quass, M. and Baumgärtner, M. (2014). "Characterizing Commercial Cattle Farms in Namibia: Risk, Management and Sustainability" Working Paper No. 248, University of Lüneburg.

85. Parker, H. and Luiz, J. (2015). "Designing Supply Chains Into Africa: A South African Retailer's Experience" In W. Piotrowicz and R. Cuthbertson (eds.), *Supply Chain Design and Management for Emerging Markets* (London: Springer), pp. 65-85.

86. Pendleton, W., Crush, J. and Nickanor, N. (2014). "Migrant Windhoek: Rural-Urban Migration and Food Security in Namibia" *Urban Forum* 25: 191-205.

87. Petersen, L. (2016). "Submission to Grocery Retail Sector Inquiry" Sustainable Livelihoods Foundation and DST-NRG Centre of Excellence in Food Security, Cape Town.

88. Peyton, S., Moseley, W. and Battersby, J. (2015). "Implications of Supermarket Expansion on Urban Food Security in Cape Town, South Africa" *African Geographical Review* 34: 36-54.

89. Pick n Pay (2016). *Pick n Pay Integrated Annual Report 2016.* At: www.picknpayinvestor.co.za/downloads/2016/PnP_IAR_2016.pdf

90. PnP (2017). "Pick n Pay Growing Local with Otavifontein" At: http://www.pnp.na/pick-n-pay-growing-local-otavifontein

91. Popkin, B. and Slining, M. (2013). "New Dynamics in Global Obesity Facing Low- and Middle-Income Countries" *Obesity Reviews* 14(S2): 11-20.

92. Popkin B., Adair, L. and Ng, S. (2012). "Global Nutrition Transition and the Pandemic of Obesity in Developing Countries" *Nutrition Reviews* 70: 3-21.

93. Reardon, T., Timmer, C., Barrett, C. and Berdegué, J. (2003). "The Rise of Supermarkets in Africa, Asia, and Latin America" *American Journal of Agricultural Economics* 85: 1140-1146.

94. Reardon, T. (2011). "The Global Rise and Impact of Supermarkets: An International Perspective" Paper for Conference on the Supermarket Revolution in Food, Canberra, Australia. At: https://ideas.repec.org/p/ags/cfcp11/125312.html

95. Reardon, T. (2015). "The Hidden Middle: The Quiet Revolution in the Midstream of Agrifood Value Chains in Developing Countries" *Oxford Review of Economic Policy* 31: 45-63.

96. Reardon, T. and Hopkins, R. (2006). "The Supermarket Revolution in Developing Countries: Policies to Address Emerging Tensions Among Supermarkets, Suppliers and Traditional Retailers" *European Journal of Development Research* 18: 522-545.

97. Reardon, T. and Minten, B. (2011). "Surprised by Supermarkets: Diffusion of Modern Food Retail in India" *Journal of Agribusiness in Developing and Emerging Economies* 1: 134-161.

98. Reardon T., Henson S. and Berdegué, J. (2007). "'Proactive Fast-Tracking' Diffusion of Supermarkets in Developing Countries: Implications for Market Institutions and Trade" *Journal of Economic Geography* 7: 399-431.

99. Reardon, T., Barrett, P., Berdegué, J. and Swinnen, J. (2009). "Agrifood Industry Transformation and Small Farmers in Developing Countries" *World Development* 37: 1717-1727.

100. Reardon, T., Timmer, C., Barrett, C. and Berdegué, J. (2003). "The Rise of Supermarkets in Africa, Asia, and Latin America" *American Journal of Agricultural Economics* 85: 1140-1146.

101. Ruel, M., Garrett, J., Yosef, S. and Olivier, M. (2017). "Urbanization, Food Security and Nutrition" In S. de Pee, D. Taren and M. Bloem (eds.), *Nutrition and Health in a Developing World* (New York: Humana Press), pp. 705-735.

102. Schipmann, C. and Qaim, M. (2011). "Modern Food Retailers and Traditional Markets in Developing Countries: Comparing Quality, Prices, and Competition Strategies in Thailand" *Applied Economic Perspectives and Policy* 33: 345-362.

103. Shoprite (2016). *Shoprite Holdings Ltd. Annual Financial Statements*, 2016. At: https://www.shopriteholdings.co.za/search-results/shop-rite-holdings-documents/financial-statements.html

104. Si, Z., Scott, S. and McCordic, C. (2016). "Supermarkets, Wet Markets and Food Patronage in Nanjing, China" HCP Discussion Paper No. 4, Waterloo.

105. Skinner, C. (2016). "Informal Food Retail in Africa: A Review of Evidence" Consuming Urban Poverty Project Working Paper No. 2, African Centre for Cities, University of Cape Town.

106. Skinner, C. and Haysom, G. (2017). "The Informal Sector's Role in Food Security: A Missing Link in Policy Debates?" HCP Discussion Paper No. 6, Waterloo and Cape Town.

107. Smit, W. (2016). "Urban Governance and Urban Food Systems in Africa: Examining the Linkages" *Cities* 58: 80-86.

108. Spar Group (2016). *The Spar Group Ltd. Integrated Report 2016*. At: https://www.spar.co.za/About-SPAR/SPAR-Financial/Annual-Reports-(1)

109. Suryadarma, D., Poesoro, A., Budiyati, S. and Rosfadhila, M. (2010). "Traditional Food Traders in Developing Countries and Competition from Supermarkets: Evidence from Indonesia" *Food Policy* 35: 79-86.

110. Thomas, B., Togarepi, C. and Simasiku, A. (2014). "Analysis of the Determinants of the Sustainability of Cattle Marketing Systems in

Zambezi Region of North-Eastern Communal Area of Namibia" *International Journal of Livestock Production* 5: 129-136.

111. Timmer, C. (2009). "Do Supermarkets Change the Food Policy Agenda?" *World Development* 37: 1812-1819.

112. Timmer, C. (2017). "The Impact of Supermarkets on Nutrition and Nutritional Knowledge: A Food Policy Perspective" In S. de Pee, D. Taren and M. Bloem (eds.), *Nutrition and Health in a Developing World* (New York: Humana Press), pp. 737-752.

113. Toiba, H., Umberger, W. and Minot, J. (2015). "Diet Transition and Supermarket Shopping Behaviour: Is There a Link?" *Bulletin of Indonesian Economic Studies* 51: 389-403.

114. Trebbin, A. (2014). "Linking Small Farmers to Modern Retail Through Producer Organizations: Experiences with Producer Companies in India" *Food Policy* 45: 35-44.

115. Tschirley, D., Reardon, T., Dolislanger, M. and Snyder, J. (2015). "The Rise of a Middle Class in East and Southern Africa: Implications for Food System Transformation" *Journal of International Development* 27: 628-646.

116. Umberger, W., He, X., Minot, N. and Toiba, H. (2015). "Examining the Relationship between the Use of Supermarkets and Over-nutrition in Indonesia" *American Journal of Agricultural Economics* 97: 510-525.

117. van der Heijden and Vink, N. (2013). "Good for Whom? Supermarkets and Small Farmers in South Africa: A Critical Review of Current Approaches to Increasing Access to Modern Markets" *Agrekon* 52: 68-86.

118. Vink, N. (2013). "Commercialising Agriculture in Africa: Economic, Social, and Environmental Impacts" *African Journal of Agricultural and Resources Economics* 9: 1-17.

119. Vorley, B., Fearne, A., and Ray, D. (2008). *Regoverning Markets: A Place for Small Scale Producers in Modern Agrifood Chains?* (London: Routledge).

120. Weatherspoon, D. and Reardon, T. (2003). "The Rise of Supermarkets in Africa: Implications for Agrifood Systems and the Rural Poor" *Development Policy Review* 21: 333-355.

121. Woolworths (2016). *Woolworths Holdings Ltd. 2016 Annual Financial Statements*. At: http://www.woolworthsholdings.co.za/investor/financial_results.asp

122. World Future Council (nd). *Growing Food in Windhoek*. At: https://www.worldfuturecouncil.org/file/2017/03/Food-Handbook-final-web.pdf

123. Zhang, Q. and Pan, Z. (2013). "The Transformation of Urban Vegetable Retail in China: Wet Markets, Supermarkets and Informal Markets in Shanghai" *Journal of Contemporary Asia* 43: 497-518.

Printed in the United States
By Bookmasters